Master Blockchain with Golang

A practical Guide to Building and Deploying Blockchain Applications using the Go Programming

Corbin Husman

Table of Contents

Preface

The world is changing at an unprecedented pace, driven by the relentless advancement of technology. At the forefront of this revolution stands blockchain, a groundbreaking innovation with the potential to reshape industries and redefine how we interact with the digital world. From cryptocurrencies like Bitcoin to decentralized applications and smart contracts, blockchain technology is rapidly transforming the way we conduct transactions, manage data, and build trust in a decentralized manner.

This book, "Master Blockchain with Golang," is your passport to this exciting new frontier. Whether you're a seasoned developer or just beginning your coding journey, this book will equip you with the knowledge and skills to harness the power of blockchain using Go, the language of choice for building scalable and efficient blockchain solutions.

Go, with its elegant syntax, powerful concurrency features, and robust standard library, is uniquely suited for the demands of blockchain development. Its speed and efficiency make it ideal for handling the complex computations and data structures inherent in blockchain technology. This book will guide you through the intricacies of Go programming, demonstrating how to leverage its strengths to build real-world blockchain applications.

Within these pages, you'll embark on a comprehensive journey, starting with the fundamental concepts of blockchain technology. You'll delve into the inner workings of cryptographic hash functions, digital signatures, and consensus mechanisms, gaining a solid understanding of the building blocks of this revolutionary technology.

From there, you'll dive into the practical aspects of blockchain development with Go. You'll learn how to construct your own blockchain, create and validate transactions, and implement smart contracts to automate complex processes. We'll explore the world of decentralized applications (DApps), guiding you through the process of building and deploying your own DApps on a blockchain network.

As you progress, you'll encounter advanced topics such as state channels, off-chain solutions, and cutting-edge cryptographic techniques, pushing the boundaries of your blockchain expertise. We'll also delve into the critical aspects of security and best practices, ensuring you build robust and resilient blockchain applications.

Finally, we'll look towards the future of blockchain with Go, exploring emerging trends and exciting new use cases. This book is not just about understanding the present; it's about empowering you to shape the future of this transformative technology.

"Master Blockchain with Golang" is more than just a technical manual; it's a gateway to a world of possibilities. With clear explanations, practical examples, and hands-on exercises, this book will guide you on your path to becoming a proficient blockchain developer. Join us on this exciting journey as we unlock the potential of blockchain with the power of Go.

Chapter 1: Introduction to Blockchain

Imagine a digital ledger, like a giant spreadsheet, shared with everyone in a network. This ledger records transactions and information in a secure and transparent way, making it nearly impossible to cheat or tamper with the data. That, in a nutshell, is blockchain.

1.1 What is Blockchain Technology?

At its core, a blockchain is a special kind of database.[1] Now, you might be thinking, "Okay, so it's just another way to store information? What's the big deal?" But here's where it gets interesting. A blockchain is not your typical database.[2] It has unique characteristics that set it apart and give it incredible power.

Think of a blockchain as a digital ledger, similar to a record book or spreadsheet, where information is recorded in a structured format. This ledger is used to store information about transactions.[3] A transaction could be anything of value – money, goods, property, even votes!

Now, here's where the "blockchain" part comes in. In a blockchain, this information is grouped together in "blocks."[4] Each block can hold a certain amount of data. Once a block is full, it's linked to the previous block, forming a "chain" of blocks.[5] This chain grows longer and longer as new blocks are added, creating a chronological record of all the transactions ever recorded on the blockchain.[6]

But there's a crucial difference between a blockchain and a regular database. In a traditional database, all the information is stored in one central location, like a company's server.[7] But a blockchain is

decentralized. This means that the information is not stored in one place but is distributed across a network of many computers.[8] Each computer in the network has a copy of the entire blockchain.[9]

This decentralized nature is what gives blockchain its remarkable properties:

- Security: Because the data is spread across many computers, it's incredibly difficult for anyone to tamper with it.[10] To alter a transaction, a hacker would need to simultaneously change the information on the majority of the computers in the network, which is practically impossible.
- Transparency: Everyone in the network can see all the transactions that have ever taken place on the blockchain.[11] This openness fosters trust and accountability.
- Immutability: Once a block of transactions is added to the blockchain, it cannot be altered or deleted.[12] This creates a permanent and auditable record of all activity.

Let's illustrate this with a simple example:

Imagine you and your friends want to keep track of who paid for what during a group trip. You could use a traditional spreadsheet, but that could be problematic. What if someone accidentally (or intentionally!) changes the numbers? With a blockchain, you can create a shared ledger where everyone can record their expenses.[13] Once an expense is recorded, it's permanently added to the chain, and no one can change it.[14] This ensures fairness and transparency for everyone involved.

Real-world example:

One of the most well-known examples of blockchain technology is **Bitcoin**.[15] Bitcoin is a cryptocurrency that uses a blockchain to record all transactions.[16] When someone sends Bitcoin to another person, that transaction is broadcast to the Bitcoin network.[17]

Miners (powerful computers on the network) then verify the transaction and add it to a block.[18] Once the block is added to the blockchain, the transaction is considered complete. This process ensures that Bitcoin transactions are secure, transparent, and tamper-proof.[19]

A simple code example (Go):

While we'll dive deeper into Go programming in the next chapter, here's a very basic example of how you can represent a block in Go code:

```
Code snippet

type Block struct {

    Timestamp      int64

    Data           []byte

    PreviousHash   string

    Hash           string

}
```

This code defines a Block structure with fields for the timestamp, the data stored in the block, the hash of the previous block, and the hash of the current block. This is a simplified representation, but it gives you a glimpse of how blockchain concepts can be translated into code.

1.2 Key Concepts

Now that you have a basic understanding of what a blockchain is, let's explore the core concepts that make this technology so unique and powerful. These concepts are like the pillars that hold up the entire blockchain structure.

Decentralization

This is a big one. For most of our digital lives, we've relied on centralized systems. Think about your bank account. All your transaction data is stored on the bank's central servers. Or consider social media platforms – your posts, photos, and messages reside on their servers. This centralized approach has some drawbacks. It creates a single point of failure. If the bank's server crashes, you might not be able to access your account. It also gives a lot of power to the central authority. They control your data and can, in theory, manipulate or even lose it.

Blockchain flips this model on its head. Instead of relying on a central authority, a blockchain distributes the information across a vast network of computers. Each computer, or "node," in the network has a copy of the entire blockchain. This means there's no single point of control. No single entity can dictate what happens on the blockchain.

Think of it like a group of friends sharing a Google Doc. Everyone has a copy of the document and can see the changes made by others. If one person's computer crashes, no problem! The document still exists on everyone else's computers.

This decentralized nature offers several advantages:

- Increased Security: With no central point of attack, it's much harder for hackers to compromise the system. They would need to simultaneously hack a majority of the nodes in the network, which is a monumental task.
- Fault Tolerance: If one or even several nodes go offline, the blockchain continues to function without interruption. This makes the system incredibly resilient.
- Greater Transparency: All the transactions on a public blockchain are visible to everyone. This openness promotes trust and accountability.

Immutability

Remember how we talked about blockchain being like a permanent record book? That's where immutability comes in. Once a block of transactions is added to the blockchain, it cannot be altered or deleted. It's like setting information in stone.

This immutability is achieved through the use of cryptographic hash functions. A hash function takes any input (like a block of transactions) and produces a unique "fingerprint" of that input, called a hash. Even a tiny change in the input will result in a completely different hash.

In a blockchain, each block contains the hash of the previous block. This creates a chain of interconnected blocks, where each block is linked to the one before it. If someone tries to tamper with a block, the hash of that block will change, breaking the chain and immediately signaling that something is wrong.

This immutability feature is crucial for many applications. For example, in supply chain management, it can be used to track the origin and movement of goods, ensuring their authenticity and preventing counterfeiting.

Transparency

In many traditional systems, data is kept hidden or is only accessible to a select few. Blockchain, on the other hand, promotes transparency. All the transactions on a public blockchain are viewable by anyone. You can think of it as a public record of all activity on the network.

This transparency has significant implications:

- Increased Trust: Because everyone can see what's happening on the blockchain, it builds trust among participants. There's no need to rely on blind faith in a central authority.

- Enhanced Accountability: If someone tries to cheat or manipulate the system, their actions will be visible to everyone. This acts as a deterrent and promotes honest behavior.
- Improved Auditability: The transparent nature of blockchain makes it easy to audit transactions and track the flow of information. This is particularly useful in industries like finance and accounting.

Real-world example:

Consider a voting system built on a blockchain. Each vote would be recorded as a transaction on the blockchain. Because the blockchain is transparent and immutable, everyone could verify that their vote was counted correctly, and no one could tamper with the results. This could lead to more secure and trustworthy elections.

Code example (Go):

While we'll explore hash functions in more detail later, here's a simple example of how you can calculate the SHA-256 hash of a string in Go:

```
Code snippet

package main

import (

    "crypto/sha256"

    "fmt"

)

func main() {
```

```go
data := "This is a string to be hashed."

hash := sha256.Sum256([]byte(data))

fmt.Printf("SHA-256 Hash: %x\n", hash)
}
```

This code snippet demonstrates how to use the sha256 package in Go to generate a hash. This is a fundamental building block for ensuring immutability in a blockchain.

Decentralization, immutability, and transparency are the cornerstones of blockchain technology. They work together to create a secure, reliable, and open system that has the potential to transform many aspects of our digital world. As you delve deeper into blockchain development, you'll see how these concepts are put into practice to create innovative and impactful applications.

1.3 Types of Blockchains

You might be surprised to learn that not all blockchains are the same. Just like there are different types of cars – sedans, SUVs, sports cars – each designed for different purposes, there are also different types of blockchains, each with its own unique characteristics and use cases. Let's explore the three main types: public, private, and permissioned.

Public Blockchains

Public blockchains are the most well-known type. Think of them as the open highways of the blockchain world. Anyone can join the network, participate in the consensus process (we'll discuss this in detail later), and view the transaction history. There are no restrictions on who can participate or what information they can access.

This openness is a defining feature of public blockchains. It fosters transparency and decentralization. Because everyone can see the transaction history, it's difficult for anyone to manipulate the data or cheat the system.

Some popular examples of public blockchains include:

- Bitcoin: The first and most famous cryptocurrency, Bitcoin uses a public blockchain to record all transactions.
- Ethereum: A platform for decentralized applications (DApps) and smart contracts, Ethereum also utilizes a public blockchain.

Key characteristics of public blockchains:

- Permissionless: Anyone can join the network and participate without needing permission from a central authority.
- Transparent: All transactions are visible to everyone on the network.
- Secure: Secured by cryptographic techniques and the decentralized nature of the network.
- Censorship-resistant: No single entity can control or censor transactions on the network.

Private Blockchains

In contrast to public blockchains, private blockchains are more like gated communities. They are controlled by a single organization or entity. Access to the network is restricted, and participants need permission to join. This makes private blockchains suitable for use cases where privacy and control are important.

For example, a company might use a private blockchain to manage its internal supply chain. Only authorized employees would be able to access and update the blockchain. This allows the company to maintain control over its data while still benefiting from the security and efficiency of blockchain technology.

Key characteristics of private blockchains:

- Permissioned: Access is restricted, and participants need authorization to join.
- Controlled: A central authority governs the network and sets the rules.
- Private: Transaction data is not visible to the public.
- Efficient: Can be more efficient than public blockchains due to the smaller number of participants.

Permissioned Blockchains

Permissioned blockchains, also known as consortium blockchains, offer a middle ground between public and private blockchains. They are like a club with membership requirements. A group of organizations might come together to create a permissioned blockchain. Access is granted to members of the consortium, but not to the general public.

This type of blockchain is often used in industries where collaboration and trust are important, such as finance or healthcare. For example, a group of banks could create a permissioned blockchain to facilitate interbank transactions. This allows them to streamline processes and reduce costs while maintaining a level of privacy and control.

Key characteristics of permissioned blockchains:

- Partially decentralized: Control is distributed among a group of organizations rather than a single entity.
- Permissioned: Access is granted to authorized participants.
- Private/Selective transparency: Transaction data might be visible only to members of the consortium or selectively shared with others.
- Efficient: Can offer a balance between efficiency and security.

Real-world examples:

- Hyperledger Fabric: An open-source framework for building permissioned blockchains, often used in enterprise applications.
- R3 Corda: A platform for building permissioned blockchains focused on financial applications.

Choosing the right type of blockchain

The choice of blockchain type depends on the specific needs and requirements of the application. Here's a quick guide to help you decide:

- Public blockchain: If you need a highly decentralized, transparent, and censorship-resistant system, a public blockchain is a good choice.
- Private blockchain: If you need to maintain control over your data and restrict access, a private blockchain is a better option.
- Permissioned blockchain: If you need a balance between privacy and collaboration, a permissioned blockchain might be the right fit.

1.4 Use Cases and Real-World Examples

By now, you're probably starting to see that blockchain is more than just a buzzword. It's a powerful technology with the potential to transform a wide range of industries.[1] Let's explore some of the most promising use cases and real-world examples of blockchain in action.

1. Cryptocurrencies

This is perhaps the most well-known application of blockchain. Cryptocurrencies like Bitcoin and Ethereum use blockchain technology to enable secure, transparent, and decentralized digital transactions.[2]

Think about how we traditionally send money. We rely on intermediaries like banks to process our transactions.[3] This can be slow, expensive, and subject to restrictions. Cryptocurrencies cut out the middleman, allowing for peer-to-peer transactions directly between individuals.[4] This can be faster, cheaper, and more accessible, especially for people in countries with limited access to traditional banking systems.[5]

Real-world example:

Consider cross-border payments. Sending money internationally through traditional channels can involve high fees and long processing times.[6] With cryptocurrencies, you can send money to someone in another country almost instantly, with significantly lower fees.[7] This has the potential to revolutionize international trade and remittances.

2. Supply Chain Management

Blockchain can be used to track goods as they move through the supply chain, from the origin of raw materials to the final product.[8] This creates a transparent and immutable record of the journey, ensuring product authenticity and preventing counterfeiting.[9]

Real-world example:

Imagine a food company using blockchain to track the origin of its ingredients.[10] Consumers could scan a QR code on the product packaging to see the entire journey of the food, from the farm where it was grown to the processing plant and finally to the store shelf.[11] This increases transparency and builds consumer trust.[12]

3. Healthcare

Blockchain can revolutionize healthcare by providing a secure and efficient way to store and share medical records.[13] This gives patients more control over their data and improves interoperability between healthcare providers.[14]

Real-world example:

A patient's medical history could be stored on a blockchain, accessible only to authorized healthcare providers.[15] This eliminates the need for patients to carry around paper records or request them from different providers. It also reduces the risk of data breaches and ensures that patients have a complete and accurate record of their medical history.[16]

4. Digital Identity

Blockchain can be used to create verifiable digital identities, simplifying identity verification processes and reducing the risk of identity theft.[17]

Real-world example:

Instead of carrying around physical documents like passports or driver's licenses, individuals could have their identity information stored securely on a blockchain.[18] This would streamline processes like opening a bank account, voting, or crossing borders.[19]

5. Voting Systems

Blockchain can create secure and transparent voting systems, reducing the risk of fraud and manipulation.[20]

Real-world example:

Each vote could be recorded as a transaction on a blockchain. This would create an immutable record of the votes cast, making it nearly impossible to tamper with the results.[21] This could lead to more trustworthy and democratic elections.

6. Intellectual Property Protection

Blockchain can be used to register and protect intellectual property rights, such as patents, copyrights, and trademarks.[22]

Real-world example:

An artist could register their artwork on a blockchain, creating a timestamped record of ownership.[23] This would make it easier to prove ownership and prevent copyright infringement.[24]

7. Real Estate

Blockchain can streamline real estate transactions by providing a secure and transparent platform for recording property ownership and transferring titles.[25]

Real-world example:

Property deeds could be stored on a blockchain, eliminating the need for paper-based records and reducing the risk of fraud.[26] This could make buying and selling property faster, cheaper, and more efficient.[27]

Code example (Go):

While specific code examples will vary depending on the use case, here's a simple illustration of how you might represent a digital asset on a blockchain using Go:

```
Code snippet

type Asset struct {

    ID          string

    Owner       string

    Description string
```

```
}
```

This code defines a structure to represent an asset with fields for its unique ID, current owner, and description. This basic structure can be expanded to include other relevant information, such as transaction history or ownership transfer records.

These are just a few examples of how blockchain is being used to solve real-world problems. As the technology continues to evolve, we can expect to see even more innovative applications emerge. By understanding the potential of blockchain and learning how to develop with Go, you'll be well-equipped to contribute to this exciting and rapidly growing field.

Chapter 2: Introduction to Golang

Okay, so we've covered the basics of blockchain. Now it's time to get our hands dirty with some code! In this chapter, we'll introduce you to Go, the programming language we'll be using throughout this book to build our own blockchain applications.

2.1 Why Go for Blockchain Development?

You might be wondering, "Why are we using Go for blockchain development? Aren't there other languages I could use?" And you'd be absolutely right! There are many programming languages out there, each with its own strengths and weaknesses. But Go, also known as Golang, has some specific characteristics that make it a particularly good fit for the unique challenges of building blockchain applications.

Let's explore why Go is gaining popularity in the blockchain space:

1. Speed and Efficiency

Go is a compiled language. This means that when you write Go code, it's translated directly into machine instructions that your computer can understand and execute. This is different from interpreted languages, where the code is executed line by line by an interpreter. Compiled languages generally run much faster because the code is already in a format that the computer can readily process.

In the world of blockchain, speed and efficiency are crucial. Blockchain applications often involve complex cryptographic operations, handling large amounts of data, and communicating across networks. Go's speed helps ensure that these operations are performed quickly and efficiently, which is essential for a smooth and responsive user experience.

2. Concurrency

Go has built-in support for concurrency. This means you can easily write programs that can perform multiple tasks seemingly at the same time. Think of it like juggling – a skilled juggler can keep multiple balls in the air simultaneously. Go allows you to write programs that can "juggle" multiple tasks, such as processing transactions, validating blocks, and communicating with other nodes on the network, all concurrently.

Concurrency is particularly important for blockchain applications because they often involve handling many requests and operations simultaneously. Go's concurrency features make it easier to write efficient and scalable blockchain applications that can handle a high volume of activity.

3. Simplicity and Readability

Go was designed with simplicity in mind. It has a clean and straightforward syntax that's easy to learn and read, even if you're new to programming. This is a significant advantage in blockchain development, where code clarity and maintainability are essential.

When you're working on a complex blockchain project, you'll often be collaborating with other developers. Go's readability makes it easier for different developers to understand and work with each other's code. This can lead to fewer errors, faster development cycles, and more maintainable codebases.

4. Strong Standard Library

Go comes with a comprehensive standard library that provides a wide range of tools and functionalities for various tasks. This includes packages for networking, cryptography, data encoding, and more. Having these tools readily available in the standard library means you don't have to rely on external libraries as much, which can simplify development and reduce dependencies.

For blockchain development, the crypto package in Go's standard library is particularly useful. It provides implementations of various cryptographic algorithms, such as hash functions (SHA-256, SHA-3), digital signatures (ECDSA, RSA), and encryption algorithms. These are essential building blocks for secure blockchain applications.

5. Growing Community and Ecosystem

Go has a vibrant and growing community of developers. This means there are plenty of online resources, tutorials, and forums where you can find help and support if you get stuck. The Go community is also actively developing open-source libraries and tools that can be used for blockchain development.

This strong community and ecosystem make it easier to get started with Go and find solutions to common challenges. It also means that Go is constantly evolving and improving, with new features and libraries being added regularly.

Real-world example:

Hyperledger Fabric, a popular open-source platform for building enterprise-grade blockchain solutions, is written in Go. This demonstrates Go's suitability for building complex and demanding blockchain applications.

Code example (Go):

Here's a simple example of how you can use the crypto/sha256 package from Go's standard library to calculate the SHA-256 hash of a string:

```Go
package main

import (
```

```go
    "crypto/sha256"

    "fmt"
)

func main() {

    data := "This is a string to be hashed"

    hash := sha256.Sum256([]byte(data))

    fmt.Printf("%x\n", hash)

}
```

This code snippet illustrates how easy it is to use Go's standard library to perform cryptographic operations, which are fundamental to blockchain technology.

Go offers a powerful combination of speed, efficiency, concurrency, simplicity, and a strong community. These features make it an excellent choice for developing robust, scalable, and.

2.2 Setting Up Your Go Development Environment

Before you start to write Go code for blockchain applications, we need to prepare our development environment. Think of this as setting up your workshop with all the necessary tools and equipment before starting a crafting project. It might seem a bit tedious at first, but trust me, a well-organized environment will make your coding experience much smoother and more enjoyable.

1. Download and Install Go

First things first, we need to get Go installed on your computer. Head over to the official Go website (https://golang.org/) and download the appropriate installation package for your operating system (Windows, macOS, or Linux). The website provides clear instructions for each operating system, so follow those carefully.

Once the download is complete, run the installer and follow the on-screen prompts. Go will be installed in a default location, typically C:\Go on Windows, /usr/local/go on macOS and Linux.

2. Set Up Your Workspace

Go uses a specific workspace structure to organize your code. This helps keep things tidy and allows Go to find your code and dependencies easily.

Here's how to set up your workspace:

- Choose a directory: Select a location on your computer where you want to create your Go workspace. This could be anywhere you prefer, such as Documents/Go or Home/Go.
- Create the directory structure: Inside your chosen workspace directory, create three subdirectories:
  - src: This is where you'll store your Go source code files (.go files).
  - pkg: This is where Go will store compiled package objects.
  - bin: This is where Go will place executable programs built from your code.

3. Set the GOPATH Environment Variable

The GOPATH environment variable is crucial. It tells Go where to find your workspace. Here's how to set it:

- Windows:
  - Open the Start Menu and search for "environment variables."
  - Click on "Edit the system environment variables."
  - Click on the "Environment Variables..." button.

- Under "System variables,"[1] click "New..."
- Enter GOPATH as the variable name and the path to your workspace directory (e.g., C:\Users\YourName\Documents\Go) as the variable value.
- Click "OK" to save the changes.
- macOS and Linux:
  - Open your shell's configuration file (e.g., .bashrc or .zshrc).
  - Add the following line, replacing /path/to/your/workspace with the actual path to your workspace:

```Bash
export GOPATH=/path/to/your/workspace
```

Save the file and restart your terminal or run source ~/.bashrc (or source ~/.zshrc) to apply the changes.

4. Choose a Code Editor or IDE

While you can technically write Go code in any plain text editor, using a dedicated code editor or Integrated Development Environment (IDE) with Go support can significantly enhance your productivity and coding experience. These tools offer features like syntax highlighting, code completion, debugging, and more.

Here are some popular choices:

- Visual Studio Code (VS Code): A free, lightweight, and highly extensible code editor with excellent Go support through the official Go extension.
- GoLand: A commercial IDE by JetBrains specifically designed for Go development, offering advanced features like refactoring, code navigation, and integrated testing.

- Sublime Text: A powerful text editor with a rich ecosystem of plugins, including Go support.
- Atom: Another popular open-source text editor with Go support through community packages.

Choose the editor that best suits your preferences and workflow.

5. Install Essential Tools

Go comes with a command-line tool called go that provides various commands for managing your Go projects. Some essential commands include:

- go get: This command downloads and installs Go packages and their dependencies.
- go build: This command compiles your Go code into an executable file.
- go run: This command compiles and runs your Go code directly.
- go test: This command runs any tests you've written for your code.

You can access these commands from your terminal or command prompt after installing Go.

Verifying the Installation

To make sure everything is set up correctly, open your terminal or command prompt and type the following command:

```
Bash


go version
```

This should display the version of Go you installed. You can also run go env to see all the Go environment variables, including GOPATH.

You have successfully set up your Go development environment. You're now ready to start writing Go code for your blockchain projects. In the next section, we'll cover some basic Go syntax and data structures to get you started.

2.3 Basic Go Syntax and Data Structures

Now that your Go development environment is all set up, let's get acquainted with the basics of the Go language itself. Don't worry if you're new to programming - Go is designed to be beginner-friendly, with a clear and concise syntax that's easy to learn and read.

Hello, World!

It's a tradition in the programming world to start with a simple program that prints "Hello, World!" to the console. Here's how you do it in Go:

```Go
package main

import "fmt"

func main() {

   fmt.Println("Hello, World!")

}
```

Let's break down this code snippet:

- package main: This line tells Go that this code belongs to the main package. Every Go program must have a main package, which serves as the entry point for execution.
- import "fmt": This line imports the fmt package from Go's standard library. This package provides functions for

formatted input and output, including the Println function we use to print text to the console.

- func main(): This line defines the main function. This is the function that Go will execute first when you run the program.
- fmt.Println("Hello, World!"): This line uses the Println function from the fmt package to print the string "Hello, World!" to the console.

To run this program, save it as a .go file (e.g., hello.go) in your workspace's src directory, then open your terminal, navigate to the directory containing the file, and run the command go run hello.go. You should see "Hello, World!" printed in your terminal.

Variables

Variables are like containers that hold data in your program. In Go, you declare a variable using the var keyword, followed by the variable name, type, and optional initial value.

```Go
var age int = 25

var name string = "Alice"

var balance float64 = 1000.50
```

In this example, we declare three variables: age of type int (integer), name of type string, and balance of type float64 (floating-point number).

Go also allows you to declare variables with type inference, where the compiler automatically determines the type based on the initial value:

```go
var city = "New York"    // type inferred as string

var pi = 3.14159         // type inferred as
float64
```

Data Structures

Data structures are ways to organize and store collections of data in your program. Go provides several built-in data structures:

- **Arrays:** An array is a fixed-size collection of elements of the same type.

```go
var numbers [5]int = [5]int{1, 2, 3, 4, 5}
```

This declares an array named numbers that can hold 5 integers.

- **Slices:** A slice is a dynamically-sized view of an underlying array. They are more flexible than arrays as they can grow or shrink as needed.

```go
var names []string = []string{"Alice", "Bob",
"Charlie"}
```

This declares a slice named that initially holds three strings.

- **Maps:** A map is a collection of key-value pairs.

```go
var ages map[string]int = map[string]int{

  "Alice": 25,
```

```go
    "Bob":     30,

}
```

This declares a map named ages that maps names (strings) to ages (integers).

- **Structs:** A struct is a user-defined type that groups together data elements of different types.

```go
Go

type Person struct {

    Name string

    Age   int

    City string

}

var p Person

p.Name = "Alice"

p.Age = 25

p.City = "New York"
```

This defines a struct named Person with fields for name, age, and city.

Control Flow

Go provides control flow statements like if-else and for loops to control the execution of your program.

- **if-else:**

```Go
if age >= 18 {

    fmt.Println("You are an adult.")

} else {

    fmt.Println("You are a minor.")

}
```

- **for loop:**

```Go
for i := 0; i < 10; i++ {

    fmt.Println(i)

}
```

This loop will print the numbers from 0 to 9.

Functions

Functions are reusable blocks of code that perform specific tasks.

```Go
func add(x int, y int) int {

    return x + y

}
```

This defines a function named add that takes two integers as input and returns their sum.

These are just the basic building blocks of Go syntax. As you progress through this book, you'll learn more advanced concepts and techniques for building blockchain applications. Remember to practice writing code and experimenting with different data structures and control flow statements to solidify your understanding.

2.4 Essential Packages for Blockchain Development

One of the great things about Go is its comprehensive standard library, which provides a rich set of tools and functionalities for various programming tasks. This means you often don't need to rely on external libraries, making your code cleaner and easier to manage. For blockchain development, several packages in the Go standard library are particularly useful. Let's explore some of these essential packages:

1. crypto

The crypto package is your go-to resource for cryptographic operations, which are fundamental to blockchain technology. It provides implementations of various cryptographic algorithms that you'll need to build secure and reliable blockchain applications.

Here are some key components of the crypto package:

- Hash functions: Hash functions are used extensively in blockchain to generate unique fingerprints of data. The crypto package provides implementations of popular hash functions like SHA-256 (used in Bitcoin) and SHA-3. You can use these functions to generate hashes of transactions, blocks, and other data to ensure integrity and immutability.
- Digital signatures: Digital signatures are used to verify the authenticity and integrity of data. The crypto package provides implementations of digital signature algorithms

like ECDSA (used in Bitcoin) and RSA. You can use these algorithms to sign transactions and verify the signatures of other participants on the network.

- Encryption algorithms: Encryption algorithms are used to protect data confidentiality. The crypto package provides implementations of encryption algorithms like AES and RSA. You can use these algorithms to encrypt sensitive data on the blockchain, ensuring that only authorized parties can access it.

Code example (Go):

Here's an example of how you can use the crypto/sha256 package to calculate the SHA-256 hash of a string:

Go

```go
package main

import (
	"crypto/sha256"
	"fmt"
)

func main() {
	data := "This is a string to be hashed"
	hash := sha256.Sum256([]byte(data))
	fmt.Printf("%x\n", hash) // Output:
4e54d2c721cbdb6a78140e4190393d16e58091c260a431800
989e5d75c4f50ce
}
```

This code calculates the SHA-256 hash of the string "This is a string to be hashed" and prints the hexadecimal representation of the hash to the console.

2. encoding/json

In blockchain applications, you'll often need to exchange data between different nodes on the network. JSON (JavaScript Object Notation) is a popular data format for this purpose because it's lightweight, human-readable, and widely supported across different programming languages.

The encoding/json package provides functions for encoding Go data structures into JSON format and decoding JSON data into Go data structures. This allows you to easily serialize and deserialize data for communication between blockchain nodes.

Code example (Go):

```Go
package main

import (
    "encoding/json"
    "fmt"
)
type Transaction struct {
    Sender    string  `json:"sender"`
    Recipient string  `json:"recipient"`
    Amount    float64 `json:"amount"`
}
func main() {
    transaction := Transaction{Sender: "Alice",
Recipient: "Bob", Amount: 10.5}
    jsonData, _ := json.Marshal(transaction)
    fmt.Println(string(jsonData)) // Output:
{"sender":"Alice","recipient":"Bob","amount":10.5
}
}
```

This code defines a Transaction struct and then uses the json.Marshal function to convert it into a JSON string.

3. net

Blockchain applications rely heavily on networking to communicate and share data between nodes. The net package provides a comprehensive set of tools for network programming in Go.

You can use the net package to create servers and clients, establish TCP and UDP connections, resolve domain names, and perform other network-related tasks. This allows you to build blockchain nodes that can communicate with each other, exchange transactions, and participate in the consensus process.

4. fmt

The fmt package provides functions for formatted input and output. While not specific to blockchain development, it's an essential package for any Go programmer. You'll use it extensively for printing messages to the console, formatting data for display, and debugging your code.

Real-world examples:

- The crypto package is used in virtually every blockchain implementation to handle cryptographic operations like hashing and signing.
- The encoding/json package is used to serialize and deserialize blockchain data for transmission over networks.
- The net package is used to build blockchain nodes that can communicate with each other and form a decentralized network.

These are just a few of the essential packages in Go's standard library that you'll find useful for blockchain development. As you progress through this book and start building your own blockchain applications, you'll become more familiar with these packages and how to use them effectively. Remember to refer to the Go documentation for detailed information and examples of each package.

Chapter 3: Core Blockchain Concepts

3.1 Cryptographic Hash Functions

Let's discuss cryptographic hash functions. They're like the workhorses of blockchain technology, quietly working behind the scenes to ensure data integrity and security. You might not see them directly, but they're essential for making blockchain work its magic.

So, what exactly is a cryptographic hash function?

Think of it like a special kind of "digital fingerprint machine." You feed it any piece of data – a text message, an image, a whole book, even an entire movie – and it produces a unique "fingerprint" of that data, called a hash. This hash is a string of characters, usually represented in hexadecimal format (a combination of numbers and letters).

Here's the fascinating part: no matter how large or small the input data is, the hash produced will always be the same size. For example, the SHA-256 hash function, which we'll discuss shortly, always produces a 256-bit hash, regardless of whether you input a single word or a massive database.

But here's the real kicker: even a tiny change in the input data – like changing a single letter in a sentence – will result in a completely different hash. This property is called **"sensitivity to change,"** and it's what makes hash functions so valuable for ensuring data integrity.

How are hash functions used in blockchain?

In blockchain, hash functions are used to create a chain of linked blocks, where each block contains a record of transactions. Here's how it works:

1. Hashing the block data: All the transactions in a block are gathered together and combined into a single piece of data. This data is then fed into a hash function, which produces a unique hash for that block. This hash is often referred to as the "block hash."
2. Linking blocks together: Each block also contains the hash of the previous block. This creates a chain of blocks, where each block is linked to the one before it through its hash. This chain is what gives blockchain its name.
3. Ensuring immutability: Because of the sensitivity to change property of hash functions, any attempt to alter a block (e.g., by tampering with a transaction) will change its hash. This, in turn, will change the hash of the next block in the chain, and so on, effectively invalidating the entire chain following the altered block. This makes it extremely difficult to tamper with data on a blockchain.

Key properties of cryptographic hash functions:

- Deterministic: The same input will always produce the same output.
- Sensitivity to change: Even a small change in the input will result in a significantly different output.
- One-way function: It's computationally infeasible to reverse the hash function and recover the original input data from the hash.
- Collision resistance: It's extremely difficult to find two different inputs that produce the same hash.

Popular hash functions in blockchain:

- SHA-256: This is one of the most widely used hash functions, and it's the one used in Bitcoin. It produces a 256-bit hash.

- SHA-3: This is a more recent hash function that is considered to be even more secure than SHA-256. It also supports variable hash lengths.
- RIPEMD-160: This hash function is often used in combination with SHA-256 in some blockchain implementations.

Code example (Go):

Here's how you can calculate the SHA-256 hash of a string in Go using the crypto/sha256 package:

```Go
package main

import (

    "crypto/sha256"

    "fmt"

)

func main() {

    data := "This is a string to be hashed"

    hash := sha256.Sum256([]byte(data))

    fmt.Printf("%x\n", hash) // Output:
4e54d2c721cbdb6a78140e4190393d16e58091c260a431800
989e5d75c4f50ce

}
```

This code first defines a string variable data containing the text to be hashed. It then uses the sha256.Sum256() function to calculate the SHA-256 hash of the data (converted to a byte array). Finally, it prints the hexadecimal representation of the hash using fmt.Printf().

Real-world examples:

- Data integrity: Hash functions are used to verify the integrity of files downloaded from the internet. You can compare the hash of the downloaded file with the hash provided by the source to ensure that the file hasn't been corrupted during download.
- Password storage: Websites often store hashes of passwords instead of the passwords themselves. This way, even if the website's database is compromised, the actual passwords remain protected.
- Digital signatures: Hash functions are used in digital signatures to create a unique fingerprint of a document, which is then encrypted with the signer's private key.

As you can see, cryptographic hash functions are a powerful tool for ensuring data integrity and security. They are a cornerstone of blockchain technology, and understanding how they work is essential for any blockchain developer.

3.2 Digital Signatures and Public Key Cryptography

Digital signatures are like the digital equivalent of your handwritten signature, but with an added layer of security and sophistication thanks to the magic of public key cryptography.

In the physical world, you use your signature to verify your identity and show that you approve of something. For example, you sign a check to authorize a payment or a contract to indicate your agreement to its terms.

Digital signatures serve a similar purpose in the digital world. They provide a way to:

- Verify the authenticity of a digital document or message: They confirm that the document or message actually came from the person who claims to have sent it.
- Ensure data integrity: They guarantee that the document or message hasn't been tampered with in transit.
- Provide non-repudiation: They prevent the sender from denying that they sent the document or message.

How do digital signatures work?

Digital signatures rely on a fascinating concept called **public key cryptography**, also known as asymmetric cryptography. In this system, each user has two keys:

- Public key: This key is like your email address – you can share it with anyone.
- Private key: This key is like your password – you keep it secret and never share it with anyone.

Here's how the magic happens:

1. Signing a document: When you want to digitally sign a document, you use your private key to create a digital signature. This signature is unique to you and the document. It's like creating a special "lock" for the document using your private key.
2. Verifying the signature: Anyone who has your public key can then use it to verify the signature. It's like using your public key to "unlock" the document and check if the lock matches. If the signature is valid, it means the document was indeed signed by you and hasn't been tampered with.

Why are digital signatures important in blockchain?

In blockchain, digital signatures are used to verify the authenticity of transactions. When you send cryptocurrency to someone, you use your private key to digitally sign the transaction. This proves that:

- You are the rightful owner of the funds being sent.
- You authorized the transaction.

This prevents anyone from forging transactions or spending your cryptocurrency without your permission.

Code example (Go):

While a full implementation of digital signatures requires more advanced concepts, here's a simplified example of how you can generate a key pair using the crypto/ecdsa package in Go:

```Go
package main

import (

    "crypto/ecdsa"

    "crypto/elliptic"

    "crypto/rand"

    "fmt"

)

func main() {

    // Generate a key pair

    privateKey, err :=
ecdsa.GenerateKey(elliptic.P256(), rand.Reader)

    if err != nil {

        panic(err)

    }
```

```
publicKey := &privateKey.PublicKey

fmt.Println("Private Key:", privateKey)

fmt.Println("Public Key:", publicKey)
}
```

This code generates an ECDSA key pair using the P-256 elliptic curve. The privateKey variable holds the private key, and the publicKey variable holds the corresponding public key.

Real-world examples:

- Email security: Digital signatures are used to verify the sender of an email and ensure that the email hasn't been tampered with.
- Software distribution: Software developers use digital signatures to sign their software packages, allowing users to verify that the software is authentic and hasn't been modified by malicious actors.
- Secure web browsing: HTTPS websites use digital certificates, which contain digital signatures, to establish a secure connection between your browser and the website.

Digital signatures are a powerful tool for ensuring security and trust in the digital world. They are an essential component of blockchain technology, allowing for secure and verifiable transactions.m

3.3 Merkle Trees and Data Structures

They might sound like something out of a fantasy novel, but they're actually a clever data structure that plays a crucial role in blockchain technology. They help ensure data integrity and efficiency, especially when dealing with large amounts of information.

Think of a Merkle tree as a special kind of "family tree" for data. It's a hierarchical structure where each "leaf" of the tree represents a piece of data, and each "branch" represents a combination of its child leaves.

Here's how it works:

1. Hashing the data: Each individual piece of data (e.g., a transaction in a blockchain) is hashed using a cryptographic hash function (like SHA-256). This creates a unique "fingerprint" for each piece of data.
2. Pairing and hashing: These individual hashes are then paired up, and the pairs are concatenated (joined together) and hashed again. This creates a new layer of hashes.
3. Repeating the process: This pairing and hashing process is repeated until you reach the top of the tree, where a single hash remains. This top hash is called the **Merkle root**.

What are the benefits of using Merkle trees in blockchain?

- Efficient data verification: Merkle trees allow you to verify the integrity of a large dataset by only checking the Merkle root. If even a single piece of data in the tree is changed, the Merkle root will also change. This makes it easy to detect any tampering.
- Space-saving: Instead of storing all the individual data pieces, you can just store the Merkle root in the block header. This saves space and makes it more efficient to verify the integrity of the entire block.
- Simplified data synchronization: Merkle trees make it easier to synchronize data across different nodes in a blockchain network. If two nodes have different versions of a block, they can compare their Merkle trees to quickly identify the discrepancies and synchronize their data.

How are Merkle trees used in blockchain?

In blockchain, Merkle trees are primarily used to summarize all the transactions in a block. Here's how:

1. Each transaction in a block is hashed.
2. These transaction hashes are paired up and hashed, then paired up again and hashed, and so on, until you get a single Merkle root.
3. This Merkle root is included in the block header.

When a node receives a new block, it can verify the integrity of all the transactions in the block by:

1. Calculating the Merkle root from the transactions in the block.
2. Comparing the calculated Merkle root with the Merkle root included in the block header.
3. If the two roots match, it means all the transactions are valid and haven't been tampered with.

Code example (Go):

Implementing a complete Merkle tree in Go can be a bit involved, but here's a simplified example to illustrate the basic idea of hashing pairs of data:

```Go
package main

import (

    "crypto/sha256"

    "fmt"

)

func main() {
```

```go
    data1 := "transaction 1"

    data2 := "transaction 2"

    hash1 := sha256.Sum256([]byte(data1))

    hash2 := sha256.Sum256([]byte(data2))

    combinedHash :=
sha256.Sum256(append(hash1[:], hash2[:]...))

    fmt.Printf("%x\n", combinedHash)

}
```

This code calculates the SHA-256 hashes of two strings (data1 and data2), representing two transactions. It then concatenates the two hashes and calculates the hash of the combined result. This represents a single step in building a Merkle tree.

Real-world examples:

- File systems: Some file systems use Merkle trees to verify data integrity and enable efficient file synchronization.
- Git version control: Git uses Merkle trees to track changes in files and ensure data integrity in repositories.
- Databases: Some databases use Merkle trees to efficiently verify data consistency and enable faster data retrieval.

Merkle trees are a powerful data structure with numerous applications in computer science. In blockchain, they play a crucial role in ensuring data integrity, efficiency, and scalability. As you continue your blockchain journey, you'll appreciate how Merkle trees contribute to the robustness and reliability of blockchain systems.

3.4 Consensus Mechanisms

Consensus mechanisms are like the decision-making processes that keep a blockchain network running smoothly. In a decentralized system like blockchain, where there's no central authority in charge, consensus mechanisms ensure that all the nodes in the network agree on a single version of the truth.[1]

Think of it like a group of friends deciding where to go for dinner. Everyone has their own preferences, but you need to reach a consensus to avoid ending up at different restaurants. Consensus mechanisms in blockchain are like the rules you agree on to make that decision fairly and efficiently.

Why are consensus mechanisms important?

In a blockchain network, consensus mechanisms are crucial for:

- Adding new blocks: They determine how new blocks are added to the blockchain and who gets to add them.[2]
- Validating transactions: They ensure that all transactions included in a block are valid and haven't been tampered with.[3]
- Preventing double-spending: They prevent malicious actors from spending the same cryptocurrency twice.[4]
- Maintaining security: They protect the blockchain from attacks and ensure its integrity.[5]

Proof-of-Work (PoW)

Proof-of-Work is one of the most common consensus mechanisms, and it's the one used in Bitcoin.[6] It's like a competition where participants (called miners) race to solve a complex mathematical puzzle.

Here's how it works:

1. Mining: Miners use powerful computers to try to find a solution to the puzzle.[7] This process is called mining.
2. Finding a solution: The first miner to find a solution broadcasts it to the network.[8]
3. Verification: Other miners verify the solution.[9] If it's correct, the miner who found the solution gets to add a new block to the blockchain and receives a reward in the form of cryptocurrency.[10]

This process is computationally intensive and requires a lot of energy, but it ensures that the blockchain is secure and that no single entity can control it.

Code example (conceptual):

While a full implementation of PoW is complex, here's a simplified example to illustrate the idea of finding a solution that meets certain criteria:

```Go
package main

import (

    "crypto/sha256"

    "fmt"

    "strconv"

)

func main() {

    data := "some data"

    nonce := 0
```

```
for {

        input := data + strconv.Itoa(nonce)

        hash := sha256.Sum256([]byte(input))

        if hash[0] == 0 { // Simplified
condition for demonstration

                fmt.Println("Solution found!
Nonce:", nonce)

                fmt.Printf("Hash: %x\n", hash)

                break

        }

        nonce++

    }

}
```

This code iterates through different values of nonce until it finds one that, when combined with the data and hashed, produces a hash that starts with a 0. This mimics the process of miners trying different solutions until they find one that meets the required criteria.

Proof-of-Stake (PoS)

Proof-of-Stake is an alternative consensus mechanism that is more energy-efficient than PoW.[11] Instead of relying on miners solving puzzles, PoS relies on validators who "stake" their cryptocurrency to participate in the consensus process.[12]

Here's how it works:

1. Staking: Validators lock up a certain amount of their cryptocurrency as a stake.[13]
2. Validator selection: The system randomly selects a validator to propose a new block based on factors like the amount of cryptocurrency they have staked and how long they have been staking.
3. Block validation: Other validators verify the proposed block.[14] If it's valid, the block is added to the blockchain, and the validator who proposed it receives a reward.

If a validator tries to cheat the system, they risk losing their stake. This incentivizes validators to act honestly and maintain the integrity of the blockchain.

Real-world examples:

- Bitcoin: Uses Proof-of-Work, making it secure but energy-intensive.[15]
- Ethereum: Transitioned from Proof-of-Work to Proof-of-Stake (known as "The Merge") to improve energy efficiency and scalability.[16]
- Cardano: Uses a Proof-of-Stake system called Ouroboros.[17]

Other Consensus Mechanisms

There are many other consensus mechanisms, each with its own advantages and disadvantages. Some popular ones include:

- Delegated Proof-of-Stake (DPoS): Token holders vote for delegates who validate transactions.[18]
- Practical Byzantine Fault Tolerance (PBFT): Used in permissioned blockchains for high transaction throughput.[19]
- Proof-of-Authority (PoA): Relies on trusted authorities to validate transactions.[20]

The choice of consensus mechanism depends on the specific needs and goals of the blockchain application.

Chapter 4: Building Your First Blockchain

It's time to put all that knowledge into practice and build our very own blockchain! Don't worry, we'll start with a simple implementation to get the hang of the core concepts. As we progress through the book, we'll add more features and complexity.

4.1 Implementing a Basic Blockchain in Go

In this section, we'll create a basic blockchain in Go. This will be a simplified version, but it will demonstrate the core concepts of how a blockchain works.

First, let's think about what a blockchain is at its most fundamental level. It's essentially a chain of blocks, linked together securely. Each block contains some data and a connection to the block before it.

So, our first task is to define what a "block" looks like in our Go code. We'll use a struct for this:

```Go
package main

import (

    "crypto/sha256"

    "encoding/hex"

    "time"
```

```
)

// Block represents a block in the blockchain

type Block struct {

    Timestamp     int64  // Represents when the
block was created

    Data          []byte // Holds the actual
data stored in the block (transactions, etc.)

    PrevBlockHash string // Stores the hash of
the previous block in the chain

    Hash          string // Stores the hash of
this block

}
```

Let's break down this Block struct:

- Timestamp: This field stores the time when the block was created. We use int64 to represent the Unix timestamp, which is the number of seconds that have elapsed since January 1, 1970 (UTC).
- Data: This field stores the actual data contained within the block. In a real-world blockchain, this would typically be a list of transactions. For our simple example, we'll just use a byte array ([]byte) to represent arbitrary data.
- PrevBlockHash: This field stores the hash of the previous block in the chain. This is what links the blocks together, forming a chain.
- Hash: This field stores the hash of the current block. This hash is calculated based on the block's timestamp, data, and the previous block's hash.

Now, let's add a function to calculate the hash of a block:

```Go
// calculateHash calculates the SHA-256 hash of
the block data

func (b *Block) calculateHash() string {

    record := string(b.Timestamp) +
string(b.Data) + b.PrevBlockHash

    h := sha256.New()

    h.Write([]byte(record))

    hashed := h.Sum(nil)

    return hex.EncodeToString(hashed)

}
```

This calculateHash() function takes a block (b) as input and calculates its hash. It does this by:

1. Concatenating the block's timestamp, data, and previous block's hash into a single string.
2. Creating a new SHA-256 hash object using sha256.New().
3. Writing the concatenated string to the hash object using h.Write().
4. Calculating the final hash using h.Sum(nil).
5. Converting the hash to a hexadecimal string using hex.EncodeToString().

Next, let's create a function to generate a new block:

```Go
// generateBlock creates a new block with the
given data
```

```
func generateBlock(oldBlock Block, data []byte)
Block {

    var newBlock Block

    t := time.Now()

    newBlock.Data = data

    newBlock.Timestamp = t.Unix()

    newBlock.PrevBlockHash = oldBlock.Hash

    newBlock.Hash = newBlock.calculateHash()

    return newBlock

}
```

This generateBlock() function takes the previous block (oldBlock) and the new block's data (data) as input. It then creates a new block with the following properties:

- Data: Set to the provided data.
- Timestamp: Set to the current Unix timestamp.
- PrevBlockHash: Set to the hash of the oldBlock.
- Hash: Calculated using the calculateHash() function.

With these building blocks in place, you've laid the foundation for your blockchain implementation. In the next sections, we'll explore how to create the genesis block, add blocks to the chain, and validate the blockchain's integrity.

4.2 Creating Blocks and Transactions

Now that we have the basic structure of a block defined, let's explore how to create blocks and the transactions they contain.

The Genesis Block

Every blockchain needs a starting point, a first block that serves as the foundation for the rest of the chain. This very first block is called the **genesis block**. It's unique because it doesn't have a previous block to link to.

Here's how we can create a genesis block in our Go code:

Go

```go
// createGenesisBlock creates the genesis block

func createGenesisBlock() Block {

    return Block{Timestamp: time.Now().Unix(),
Data: []byte("Genesis Block"), PrevBlockHash: "",
Hash: ""}

}
```

In this function, we create a new Block with the following properties:

- Timestamp: Set to the current Unix timestamp.
- Data: Set to the string "Genesis Block" as a byte array.
- PrevBlockHash: Set to an empty string since there's no previous block.
- Hash: We don't need to explicitly calculate the hash here because the generateBlock() function will take care of that when we add the next block.

Creating a Blockchain Instance

Now, let's create a Blockchain struct to hold our chain of blocks:

Go

```go
// Blockchain represents the blockchain

type Blockchain struct {
```

```go
    chain []Block

}
```

This Blockchain struct simply has a chain field, which is a slice of Block structs. This slice will hold all the blocks in our blockchain.

To initialize a new blockchain with the genesis block, we can create a function like this:

Go

```go
// NewBlockchain creates a new blockchain with
the genesis block

func NewBlockchain() *Blockchain {

    return &Blockchain{chain:
[]Block{createGenesisBlock()}}

}
```

This NewBlockchain() function creates a new Blockchain instance and initializes its chain with the genesis block.

Transactions

In a real-world blockchain, blocks would contain transactions. A transaction represents a transfer of value between two parties. For example, in a cryptocurrency blockchain, a transaction might represent sending some coins from one address to another.

For our simplified example, we're just storing arbitrary data in the Data field of our blocks. However, let's take a quick look at how you might represent a transaction in Go:

Go

```go
type Transaction struct {
```

```go
    Sender      string   `json:"sender"`

    Recipient  string    `json:"recipient"`

    Amount     float64  `json:"amount"`

}
```

This Transaction struct has fields for the sender, recipient, and amount of a transaction. The json:"..." tags are used to specify how the struct fields should be encoded and decoded in JSON format, which is often used for communication in blockchain applications.

Adding Transactions to Blocks (Conceptual)

In a real blockchain, you would typically:

1. Create transactions.
2. Gather a set of transactions into a block.
3. Calculate the Merkle root of the transactions (we'll cover Merkle trees in a later chapter).
4. Include the Merkle root in the block header.

For our simplified example, we're skipping the Merkle tree part and just adding data directly to the Data field of the block.

Example Usage

Here's how you might use the code we've written so far:

Go

```go
func main() {

    bc := NewBlockchain()

    // Add some blocks (with simplified "data"
for now)
```

```
    bc.AddBlock("Send 1 BTC to Alice")

    bc.AddBlock("Send 2 BTC to Bob")

    // Print the blockchain data

    for _, block := range bc.chain {

        fmt.Printf("Prev. hash: %x\n",
block.PrevBlockHash)

        fmt.Printf("Data: %s\n", block.Data)

        fmt.Printf("Hash: %x\n", block.Hash)

        fmt.Println()

    }

}
```

This[1] code creates a new blockchain, adds two blocks with some sample data, and then prints the details of each block.

4.3 Adding Blocks to the Chain

Now that we have our blockchain initialized with the genesis block, let's explore how to add new blocks to the chain. This is a fundamental operation in any blockchain, as it allows the chain to grow and record new data.

The AddBlock() Function

To add a new block, we'll create a function called AddBlock() that takes the data for the new block as input. Here's the implementation:

```Go
// AddBlock adds a new block to the blockchain

func (bc *Blockchain) AddBlock(data string) {

    prevBlock := bc.chain[len(bc.chain)-1]

    newBlock := generateBlock(prevBlock,
[]byte(data))

    bc.chain = append(bc.chain, newBlock)

}
```

Let's break down this function step by step:

1. **Get the previous block:** prevBlock :=
   bc.chain[len(bc.chain)-1]

This line retrieves the last block in the chain. We use len(bc.chain)-1 to get the index of the last element in the chain slice.

2. **Generate the new block:** newBlock :=
   generateBlock(prevBlock, []byte(data))

This line uses the generateBlock() function we defined earlier to create a new block. We pass the prevBlock as the previous block and the data (converted to a byte array) as the data for the new block.

3. **Add the new block to the chain:** bc.chain =
   append(bc.chain, newBlock)

This line appends the newBlock to the chain slice, effectively adding it to the end of the blockchain.

When we add a new block, we're essentially creating a new link in the chain. The generateBlock() function takes care of linking the new block to the previous block by setting the PrevBlockHash field of the new block to the hash of the previous block. This creates a secure and tamper-proof chain of blocks.

Example Usage

Here's how you can use the AddBlock() function to add some blocks to your blockchain:

Go

```go
func main() {

    bc := NewBlockchain()

    bc.AddBlock("Send 1 BTC to Alice")

    bc.AddBlock("Send 2 BTC to Bob")

    // ... (print the blockchain data)

}
```

This code creates a new blockchain, adds two blocks with some sample data, and then you can print the details of each block as shown in the previous section.

Real-World Analogy

Think of adding blocks to a blockchain like adding new entries to a ledger. Each block is like a page in the ledger, and the PrevBlockHash is like a reference to the previous page. This ensures that all the pages are linked together in a specific order and that no one can tamper with the entries without breaking the chain.

In a real-world blockchain, adding blocks is typically a more complex process involving consensus mechanisms, transaction validation, and other factors. However, this simplified implementation demonstrates the core concept of how blocks are added to a chain.

4.4 Validating the Blockchain

We've built a basic blockchain and added some blocks to it. But how can we be sure that our blockchain is valid and hasn't been tampered with? That's where validation comes in.

Think of validation as a security check for your blockchain. It's like having a guard at the gate, ensuring that only legitimate blocks are allowed into the chain. This is crucial for maintaining the integrity and trustworthiness of your blockchain.

In a decentralized system like blockchain, where there's no central authority controlling things, anyone can potentially add blocks to the chain.[1] This openness is a strength of blockchain, but it also means that we need mechanisms to prevent malicious actors from adding invalid or fraudulent blocks.

Validation helps us achieve this by:

- Ensuring data integrity: It verifies that the data within each block hasn't been altered.
- Detecting tampering: It identifies any attempts to modify the blockchain's history.
- Maintaining consistency: It ensures that all nodes in the network agree on the same valid blockchain.

How do we validate a blockchain?

To validate a blockchain, we need to check each block in the chain and ensure that it meets certain criteria. Here are the key checks we perform:

1. Previous block hash: We check if the PrevBlockHash field of the current block matches the hash of the previous block. This ensures that the blocks are correctly linked together in a chain.
2. Block hash: We recalculate the hash of the current block using the calculateHash() function and compare it with the Hash field stored in the block. This ensures that the block's data hasn't been tampered with.

Implementing validation in Go

Let's create a function called isBlockValid() to perform these checks:

Go

```go
// isBlockValid checks if a block is valid
compared to its predecessor

func isBlockValid(newBlock, oldBlock Block) bool
{

    if oldBlock.Hash != newBlock.PrevBlockHash {

        return false

    }

    if newBlock.calculateHash() != newBlock.Hash
{

        return false

    }

    return true

}
```

This function takes two blocks as input: the new block being validated and the previous block in the chain. It performs the following checks:

- if oldBlock.Hash != newBlock.PrevBlockHash: It checks if the PrevBlockHash of the new block matches the Hash of the old block. If they don't match, it means the link between the blocks is broken, and the function returns false.
- if newBlock.calculateHash() != newBlock.Hash: It recalculates the hash of the new block using the calculateHash() function and compares it with the Hash field stored in the block. If they don't match, it means the block's data has been tampered with, and the function returns false.

If both checks pass, the function returns true, indicating that the block is valid.

Validating the entire chain

To validate the entire blockchain, you would typically iterate through the blocks in the chain, starting from the genesis block, and call the isBlockValid() function for each consecutive pair of blocks.

Real-world example

Think of validating a blockchain like checking the authenticity of a historical document. You might examine the seals, signatures, and handwriting to ensure that the document is genuine and hasn't been forged or altered. Similarly, validating a blockchain ensures that the data it holds is authentic and trustworthy.

In a real-world blockchain, validation often involves more complex checks, such as verifying digital signatures, checking transaction validity, and enforcing consensus rules. However, this simplified implementation demonstrates the core concept of blockchain validation.

By implementing validation, you add a crucial layer of security to your blockchain, ensuring its integrity and trustworthiness. This is essential for building reliable and secure blockchain applications.

Chapter 5: Working with Smart Contracts

5.1 Introduction to Smart Contracts

They're a fascinating and powerful element of blockchain technology, often described as "self-executing contracts" or "programmable agreements."[1] But what exactly are they, and how do they work?

Think of a smart contract as a computer program that automatically enforces the terms of an agreement.[2] It's like having a digital lawyer built directly into the system, ensuring that all parties involved uphold their end of the deal.

Here's a breakdown of the key characteristics of smart contracts:

- Self-executing: Once a smart contract is deployed on a blockchain, it automatically executes its code according to predefined rules and conditions.[3] There's no need for manual intervention or reliance on third parties to enforce the agreement.[4]
- Immutable: The code of a smart contract, once deployed, cannot be altered or tampered with.[5] This ensures that the terms of the agreement remain fixed and cannot be changed without the consent of all parties involved.[6]
- Transparent: The code and execution of a smart contract are visible to everyone on the blockchain network.[7] This transparency promotes trust and accountability, as all participants can verify the contract's logic and execution.[8]
- Decentralized: Smart contracts operate on a decentralized blockchain network, meaning they are not controlled by any single entity. This eliminates single points of failure and censorship, making them more resilient and resistant to manipulation.[9]

How Smart Contracts Work

Let's walk through a typical lifecycle of a smart contract:

1. Creation: A developer writes the smart contract code, defining the rules, conditions, and actions that will be executed.[10] This code is often written in specialized languages like Solidity (for Ethereum) or Vyper.[11]
2. Compilation: The code is then compiled into bytecode, a low-level representation that can be understood and executed by the blockchain's virtual machine.[12]
3. Deployment: The compiled bytecode is deployed to a blockchain network through a transaction.[13] This transaction creates a unique address on the blockchain where the smart contract resides.
4. Trigger: The smart contract waits for an event or transaction that triggers its execution.[14] This could be something like receiving a payment, reaching a specific date, or receiving data from an external source.
5. Execution: When triggered, the smart contract's code is executed by the blockchain's virtual machine.[15] This execution can involve various actions, such as transferring funds between addresses, updating data on the blockchain, or interacting with other smart contracts.[16]

Real-World Examples

Smart contracts have the potential to revolutionize a wide range of industries.[17] Here are a few examples:

- Decentralized Finance (DeFi): Smart contracts are used to create decentralized lending platforms, stablecoins, decentralized exchanges, and other financial instruments.[18] They automate processes, reduce reliance on intermediaries, and increase transparency in financial transactions.[19]

- Supply Chain Management: Smart contracts can track goods as they move through a supply chain, automatically release payments when goods are delivered, and verify product authenticity.[20] This improves efficiency, reduces fraud, and increases transparency in supply chains.
- Gaming: Smart contracts can be used to create unique in-game assets, manage ownership of those assets, and facilitate fair gameplay.[21] This enables new forms of digital ownership and creates more engaging and transparent gaming experiences.[22]
- Healthcare: Smart contracts can securely store and share medical records, automate insurance claims processing, and manage clinical trials.[23] This improves data privacy, streamlines healthcare processes, and enhances trust between patients and providers.[24]
- Real Estate: Smart contracts can automate property transactions, manage rental agreements, and track property ownership.[25] This reduces paperwork, speeds up transactions, and increases transparency in the real estate market.[26]

Benefits of Smart Contracts

Smart contracts offer several advantages over traditional contracts:

- Increased efficiency: They automate processes, reducing the time and costs associated with manual execution and enforcement.[27]
- Enhanced security: Immutability and transparency make them resistant to fraud and tampering.[28]
- Reduced costs: They eliminate the need for intermediaries, such as lawyers and banks, reducing transaction costs.[29]
- Improved trust and transparency: All parties can view the contract's code and execution, fostering trust and accountability.[30]

As you can see, smart contracts are a powerful tool for automating agreements and processes on the blockchain.[31] They have the potential to transform various industries and create new possibilities for innovation and efficiency.[32] In the following sections, we'll explore how to write and interact with smart contracts using Go.

5.2 Writing Smart Contracts in Go

While Go isn't the primary language for writing the core logic of smart contracts (languages like Solidity are more commonly used for that), it plays a crucial role in the broader ecosystem of smart contract development and interaction.

Think of it this way: Solidity is like the language you use to write the blueprint for a building, while Go is like the set of tools and machinery you use to construct that building and interact with it once it's built.

Here's how Go fits into the world of smart contracts:

1. Building Applications that Interact with Smart Contracts

Go excels at building applications that interact with smart contracts deployed on a blockchain. You can use Go to:

- Connect to blockchain nodes: Go provides libraries and tools to connect to blockchain nodes, which are the computers that maintain the blockchain network. This allows your Go applications to communicate with the blockchain and access smart contract functionality.
- Send transactions: You can use Go to create and send transactions to the blockchain. These transactions can trigger smart contract functions, transfer digital assets, or update data on the blockchain.

- Read data from smart contracts: Go allows you to read data stored in smart contracts, such as the current state of a contract or the results of its execution.

2. Deploying Smart Contracts

Although you typically write the smart contract code itself in a language like Solidity, you can use Go to handle the deployment process. Go libraries provide functions to:

- Compile Solidity code: Convert Solidity code into bytecode that can be understood by the blockchain's virtual machine.
- Create deployment transactions: Package the compiled bytecode into a transaction that deploys the smart contract to the blockchain.
- Send deployment transactions: Broadcast the deployment transaction to the blockchain network.

3. Generating Go Bindings for Smart Contracts

To interact with a smart contract from your Go code, you need a way to represent the contract's functions and data structures in Go. The abigen tool, included with the go-ethereum library, helps you do this.

abigen takes a smart contract's ABI (Application Binary Interface) as input and generates Go code that represents the contract's interface. This generated code allows you to easily call the contract's functions and access its data from your Go applications.

Example: Generating Go Bindings

Let's say you have a simple Solidity smart contract called SimpleStorage:

```
Solidity

pragma solidity ^0.8.0;
```

```
contract SimpleStorage {

    uint storedData;

    function set(uint x) public {

        storedData = x;

    }

    function get() public view returns (uint) {

        return storedData;

    }

}
```

You can[1] use abigen to generate Go bindings for this contract:

Bash

```
abigen --abi SimpleStorage.abi --pkg main --out
simplesstorage.go
```

This command will generate a Go file (simplesstorage.go) that contains Go representations of the SimpleStorage contract's functions (set and get) and its data (storedData).

Interacting with the Smart Contract from Go

Once you have the Go bindings, you can use them to interact with the smart contract from your Go code. Here's a conceptual example:

Go

```
// ... (import necessary libraries)
```

```
// ... (connect to a blockchain node)

// ... (deploy the SimpleStorage contract)

// ... (create an instance of the SimpleStorage
contract using the generated bindings)

// ... (call the set() function to store a value)

// ... (call the get() function to retrieve the
stored value)
```

This example outlines the general steps involved in interacting with a smart contract from Go. We'll explore these steps in more detail and with concrete examples in later chapters as we build more complex blockchain applications.

Real-World Examples

- Gnosis Safe: A popular multi-signature wallet that uses Go for its backend infrastructure, interacting with smart contracts to manage digital assets securely.
- Chainlink: A decentralized oracle network that uses Go to connect smart contracts to real-world data and APIs.

By understanding how Go can be used to write applications that interact with, deploy, and manage smart contracts, you gain a valuable skill set for building robust and sophisticated blockchain solutions. While Go might not be the language you use to write the smart contract logic itself, it's an indispensable tool for integrating smart contracts into real-world applications.

5.3 Deploying and Interacting with Smart Contracts

Let's discuss the practical aspects of working with smart contracts. We'll explore how to deploy them onto a blockchain and how to interact with them using Go.

Deploying a Smart Contract

Think of deploying a smart contract like launching a spacecraft. You've built this incredible piece of technology (your smart contract code), and now it's time to send it out into the blockchain universe.

Here's a breakdown of the deployment process:

1. **Prepare the Contract:**
   - Write the code: You'll typically write your smart contract in a language like Solidity.[1]
   - Compile: Use a Solidity compiler (like solc) to compile your code into bytecode, a low-level representation that the blockchain's virtual machine can understand.
2. **Connect to a Blockchain Node:**
   - You'll need to connect to a node on the blockchain network where you want to deploy your contract.[2] This node acts as your gateway to the blockchain.
   - Go libraries like go-ethereum provide functions to establish connections to Ethereum nodes.
3. **Create a Deployment Transaction:**
   - A transaction is like a message that you send to the blockchain. To deploy a smart contract, you create a special kind of transaction that includes the compiled bytecode of your contract.[3]

- This transaction also specifies other details, such as the amount of gas (transaction fee) you're willing to pay and any initial values for the contract's storage.

4. **Sign the Transaction:**
   - You need to sign the transaction with your private key to prove that you're authorized to deploy the contract. This is like adding your digital signature to a document.

5. **Send the Transaction:**
   - Broadcast the signed transaction to the blockchain network through the connected node.

6. **Wait for Confirmation:**
   - The blockchain network will process your transaction and include it in a block.[4] Once the block is added to the blockchain, your contract is officially deployed!

Interacting with a Deployed Smart Contract

Once your smart contract is deployed, you can interact with it by sending transactions to its address.[5] These transactions can:

- Call Functions: Trigger functions defined in the smart contract code. For example, if your contract has a function called transferFunds(), you can send a transaction to call that function and transfer funds between addresses.
- Send Data: Provide data as input to the contract's functions.[6] For example, if your contract has a function called updateRecord(string memory newRecord), you can send a transaction with the newRecord data to update a record on the blockchain.
- Read Data: Retrieve data stored in the contract's state. For example, if your contract stores a value called totalSupply, you can send a transaction to read that value.

Go Libraries for Smart Contract Interaction

Go provides several libraries to help you interact with smart contracts:[7]

- **go-ethereum**: The official Go implementation of the Ethereum protocol.[8] It provides a comprehensive set of functions for interacting with Ethereum nodes and smart contracts.[9]
- **abigen**: A tool included with go-ethereum that generates Go bindings for Solidity smart contracts. This makes it easier to call contract functions and access data from your Go code.

Example (Conceptual)

Here's a conceptual example of how you might interact with a simple smart contract using Go:

```Go
// ... (import necessary libraries, including
go-ethereum and the generated bindings for your
contract)

// ... (connect to an Ethereum node)

// ... (get an instance of your contract using
its address and the generated bindings)

// ... (create a transaction to call a function
in the contract)

// ... (sign the transaction with your private
key)

// ... (send the transaction to the network)

// ... (wait for the transaction to be mined)

// ... (read the result of the function call)
```

This example outlines the general steps involved in interacting with a smart contract using Go. We'll explore these steps in more detail and with concrete examples in later chapters as we build more complex blockchain applications.

Real-World Examples

- Augur: A decentralized prediction market platform that uses Go for its backend infrastructure, allowing users to create and participate in prediction markets through smart contracts.
- MakerDAO: A decentralized organization that uses Go to manage its Dai stablecoin system, which relies on smart contracts to maintain the stability of the Dai token.

By understanding how to deploy and interact with smart contracts using Go, you gain a valuable skill set for building and integrating decentralized applications. Whether you're building a DeFi platform, a supply chain solution, or a decentralized game, Go provides the tools and libraries you need to interact with the world of smart contracts.[10]

Chapter 6: Developing Decentralized Applications

6.1 Understanding DApp Architecture

Let's talk about decentralized applications, or DApps. You might have heard the term thrown around, but what exactly are they? Essentially, a DApp is an application that runs on a decentralized network, like a blockchain. It's like a traditional application, but with the added benefits of blockchain technology – things like transparency, security, and immutability.

Key Components of a DApp

To understand how DApps work, let's break down their key components:

1. **Frontend**

The frontend is the part of the DApp that users interact with directly. It's what they see and use to perform actions within the application. Think of it like the user interface of a website or a mobile app. The frontend of a DApp can be built using the same technologies used for traditional web applications, such as:

- ○ HTML: For structuring the content of the application.
- ○ CSS: For styling the appearance of the application.
- ○ JavaScript: For adding interactivity and dynamic behavior to the application.

2. **Smart Contracts**

Smart contracts are the brains of a DApp. They contain the application's logic and define how it functions. They're like automated agreements written in code that execute when specific conditions are met. Smart contracts are typically written in languages like Solidity (for Ethereum) or Vyper. They are deployed onto a blockchain, where they become immutable and transparent.

3. **Blockchain**

The blockchain is the foundation upon which the DApp is built. It provides a decentralized and secure platform for storing the smart contracts, recording transactions, and managing the application's data. Different DApps might use different blockchain platforms, depending on their specific needs and requirements. Some popular platforms include Ethereum, Hyperledger Fabric, and EOS.

4. **Data Storage**

While some data can be stored directly on the blockchain, it's often not suitable for storing large amounts of data or complex data structures. This is because storing data on the blockchain can be expensive and can affect the network's performance. Therefore, DApps often use off-chain data storage solutions to store larger or more complex data. Some popular options include:

- IPFS (InterPlanetary File System): A peer-to-peer distributed file system that allows you to store and access files in a decentralized manner.
- Swarm: A decentralized storage platform that is part of the Ethereum ecosystem.

How DApps Differ from Traditional Apps

Here are some key distinctions between DApps and traditional applications:

Feature	DApp	Traditional App

Backend	Blockchain and smart contracts	Centralized servers
Control	Decentralized, no single entity in charge	Controlled by a single entity
Transparency	High, code and data often public	Low, code and data usually private
Security	Cryptographically secure	Reliant on server security
Data Integrity	High, data is immutable	Susceptible to data breaches

Real-World Examples

To better understand DApp architecture, let's look at some real-world examples:

- Uniswap: A decentralized exchange (DEX) built on Ethereum that allows users to trade cryptocurrencies without intermediaries. Its smart contracts handle the trading logic, and its frontend provides a user interface for interacting with the exchange.
- Compound Finance: A decentralized lending platform that allows users to earn interest on their cryptocurrencies or borrow cryptocurrencies against their holdings. Its smart contracts manage the lending and borrowing processes, and its frontend provides a user interface for interacting with the platform.
- Axie Infinity: A popular blockchain-based game that uses NFTs (non-fungible tokens) to represent in-game creatures. Its smart contracts manage the ownership and breeding of these creatures, and its frontend provides a gaming interface for players.

Understanding DApp architecture is crucial for developing and working with decentralized applications. By combining the power of blockchain technology with traditional application development principles, DApps offer a new paradigm for building secure, transparent, and user-friendly applications.

6.2 Building a Simple DApp with Go

This will be a basic example, but it will give you a taste of how Go can be used to interact with smart contracts and the blockchain.

Our Simple DApp: A Counter

For this example, we'll create a DApp that interacts with a smart contract that stores a simple counter. Our DApp will have two main functions:

- Increment: Increases the counter value by 1.
- Get: Retrieves the current counter value and displays it in the frontend.

Prerequisites

Before we start, make sure you have the following:

- Go development environment: You should have Go installed and your GOPATH set up correctly (refer to Chapter 2 if you need a refresher).
- go-ethereum library: Install the go-ethereum library using go get github.com/ethereum/go-ethereum.
- Solidity compiler: Install the Solidity compiler (solc).
- An Ethereum node: You can either run your own Ethereum node or use a node provider service like Infura or Alchemy.

1. The Smart Contract

First, we need to write the Solidity code for our counter contract:

```solidity
Solidity

pragma solidity ^0.8.0;

contract Counter {

    uint256 public count = 0;

    function increment() public {

        count++;

    }

    function getCount() public view returns
(uint256) {

        return count;

    }

}
```

This simple contract has a state variable count that stores the counter value. The increment() function increases the counter by 1, and the getCount() function returns the current counter value.

2. Compile the Contract

Compile the Solidity code using solc:

```bash
Bash

solc --abi --bin Counter.sol -o ./
```

This will generate two files: Counter.abi (the contract's ABI) and Counter.bin (the compiled bytecode).

3. Generate Go Bindings

Use abigen to generate Go bindings for the contract:

Bash

```bash
abigen --abi Counter.abi --pkg main --out
counter.go
```

This will generate a Go file (counter.go) that contains Go representations of the Counter contract's functions and data.

4. The Go Code

Now, let's write the Go code for our DApp:

Go

```go
package main

import (

    "context"

    "fmt"

    "log"

    "math/big"


"github.com/ethereum/go-ethereum/accounts/abi/bind"

    "github.com/ethereum/go-ethereum/common"

    "github.com/ethereum/go-ethereum/crypto"

    "github.com/ethereum/go-ethereum/ethclient"

)
```

```go
// ... (Your Counter contract bindings from
counter.go)

func main() {

    // Connect to an Ethereum node

    client, err :=
ethclient.Dial("YOUR_ETHEREUM_NODE_URL")

    if err != nil {

        log.Fatal(err)

    }

    // Load your private key

    privateKey, err :=
crypto.HexToECDSA("YOUR_PRIVATE_KEY")

    if err != nil {

        log.Fatal(err)

    }

    // Get the public key and address

    publicKey := privateKey.Public()

    publicKeyECDSA, ok :=
publicKey.(*ecdsa.PublicKey)

    if !ok {

        log.Fatal("error casting public key to
ECDSA")

    }
```

```go
    fromAddress :=
crypto.PubkeyToAddress(*publicKeyECDSA)

    // Get the nonce

    nonce, err :=
client.PendingNonceAt(context.Background(),
fromAddress)

    if err != nil {

        log.Fatal(err)

    }

    // Create a transaction signer

    gasPrice, err :=
client.SuggestGasPrice(context.Background())

    if err != nil {

        log.Fatal(err)

    }

    auth := bind.NewKeyedTransactor(privateKey)

    auth.Nonce = big.NewInt(int64(nonce))

    auth.Value = big.NewInt(0) // in wei

    auth.GasLimit = uint64(3000000) // in units

    auth.GasPrice = gasPrice

    // Deploy the contract

    address, tx, instance, err :=
DeployCounter(auth, client)
```

```go
	if err != nil {

		log.Fatal(err)

	}

	fmt.Println("Contract deployed to address:",
address.Hex())

	fmt.Println("Transaction hash:",
tx.Hash().Hex())

	// Wait for the transaction to be mined

	_, err =
bind.WaitDeployed(context.Background(), client,
tx)

	if err != nil {

		log.Fatal(err)

	}

	// Interact with the contract

	fmt.Println("Initial count:",
instance.Count(nil))

	tx, err = instance.Increment(auth)

	if err != nil {

		log.Fatal(err)

	}

	fmt.Println("Increment transaction hash:",
tx.Hash().Hex())
```

```go
    // Wait for the transaction to be mined

    _, err =
bind.WaitMined(context.Background(), client, tx)

    if err != nil {

        log.Fatal(err)

    }

    fmt.Println("Count after increment:",
instance.Count(nil))

}
```

This code does the following:

- Connects to an Ethereum node.
- Loads your private key.
- Deploys the Counter contract.
- Interacts with the contract by calling the increment() and getCount() functions.

5. The Frontend

You can create a simple HTML frontend with buttons to trigger the increment() and get() functions. You'll need to use JavaScript and a library like Web3.js to interact with the Go backend and the smart contract.

Real-World Examples

- Decentralized voting systems: Go can be used to build the backend of a DApp that allows users to cast votes securely and transparently on a blockchain.
- Supply chain tracking applications: Go can be used to create a DApp that tracks the movement of goods through a supply

chain, recording each step on the blockchain for transparency and accountability.

This simple DApp demonstrates how Go can be used to interact with smart contracts and the blockchain. As you gain more experience, you can build more complex DApps with richer functionalities, leveraging the power of Go and blockchain technology to create innovative and decentralized solutions.

6.3 Connecting Your DApp to a Blockchain

Let's discuss the crucial step of connecting your decentralized application (DApp) to a blockchain. This connection is what allows your DApp to leverage the power of blockchain technology – things like decentralization, security, and transparency.

Think of it like plugging your DApp into a global network of computers that maintain the blockchain. This connection enables your DApp to interact with smart contracts, send and receive transactions, and access data stored on the blockchain.

1. Choose a Blockchain Platform

The first step is to choose the blockchain platform that best suits your DApp's needs. There are various blockchain platforms available, each with its own strengths and weaknesses. Some popular options include:

- Ethereum: A widely used platform for DApps and smart contracts, known for its large community and robust ecosystem.
- Hyperledger Fabric: An enterprise-focused platform that offers features like privacy and permissioned access, suitable for business applications.
- EOS: A high-performance platform that boasts fast transaction speeds and scalability, making it suitable for applications that require high throughput.

- Polygon: A layer-2 scaling solution for Ethereum that offers faster and cheaper transactions, making it a good choice for DApps that require frequent interactions.

Consider factors like transaction costs, scalability, security, and community support when choosing a platform.

2. Set Up a Node

To interact with a blockchain, you need to connect to a node on the network. A node is a computer that runs the blockchain software and maintains a copy of the blockchain data.

You have two main options for setting up a node:

- Run your own node: This gives you full control over your node but requires technical expertise and resources to set up and maintain.
- Use a node provider service: Services like Infura, Alchemy, and Quicknode provide access to blockchain nodes, eliminating the need for you to run your own. This is often a more convenient option, especially for development and smaller projects.

3. Use a Go Library

Go offers several libraries that simplify interacting with blockchains. These libraries provide functions for:

- Connecting to nodes: Establish connections to blockchain nodes using various protocols (e.g., JSON-RPC, WebSockets).
- Sending transactions: Create, sign, and send transactions to the blockchain.
- Interacting with smart contracts: Call functions, send data, and read data from smart contracts.

Some popular Go libraries for blockchain interaction include:

- go-ethereum: The official Go implementation of the Ethereum protocol, providing comprehensive support for interacting with Ethereum nodes and smart contracts.
- go-web3: A Go library for interacting with the Web3 API, which is a standard interface for interacting with Ethereum and other EVM-compatible blockchains.

4. Handle Authentication

If your DApp involves user accounts and private data, you'll need to implement secure authentication mechanisms. This typically involves:

- User registration and login: Allow users to create accounts and securely log in to your DApp.
- Wallet integration: Integrate with cryptocurrency wallets (like MetaMask) to allow users to manage their digital assets and sign transactions.
- Access control: Implement access control rules to restrict access to sensitive data and functionalities based on user roles and permissions.

5. Manage Transactions

Interacting with a blockchain often involves sending transactions. Your DApp needs to handle:

- Transaction creation: Construct transactions that specify the actions to be performed on the blockchain (e.g., calling a smart contract function, transferring funds).
- Transaction signing: Sign transactions with the user's private key to authorize the actions.
- Transaction sending: Broadcast signed transactions to the blockchain network through the connected node.
- Transaction monitoring: Track the status of sent transactions and handle confirmations or errors.

Real-World Examples

- Brave Browser: A privacy-focused web browser that uses Go for its backend infrastructure, connecting to the Ethereum blockchain to reward users with BAT (Basic Attention Token) for viewing ads.
- Decentraland: A virtual world platform that uses Go to connect to the Ethereum blockchain, allowing users to buy, sell, and develop virtual land and assets.

By following these steps and using the appropriate Go libraries, you can connect your DApp to a blockchain and leverage its capabilities to build decentralized, secure, and transparent applications. Remember to choose the right blockchain platform and node provider for your specific needs and implement robust authentication and transaction management mechanisms to ensure the security and reliability of your DApp.

Chapter 7: Advanced Blockchain Concepts

You've mastered the basics of blockchain and built your first DApp. Now, let's push the boundaries and explore some advanced concepts that will deepen your understanding and expand your blockchain toolkit.

7.1 Exploring Different Consensus Mechanisms

We've already touched on the importance of consensus mechanisms in blockchain – they're the rules that ensure everyone in the network agrees on a single version of the truth. But the world of consensus mechanisms extends far beyond the Proof-of-Work (PoW) and Proof-of-Stake (PoS) we discussed earlier.

Think of consensus mechanisms as different ways to govern a blockchain network. Just like different countries have different forms of government, different blockchains use different consensus mechanisms to achieve their specific goals and priorities.

Each consensus mechanism has its own set of trade-offs and advantages. Some prioritize security above all else, while others focus on speed, scalability, or energy efficiency. Understanding these trade-offs allows you to choose the right mechanism for your specific blockchain application.

Let's explore some popular consensus mechanisms beyond PoW and PoS:

1. Delegated Proof-of-Stake (DPoS)

DPoS is like a representative democracy for blockchains. Instead of every node participating directly in the consensus process, token holders vote for delegates (also called witnesses or block producers) who are responsible for validating transactions and adding blocks to the chain.

Think of it like electing representatives to make decisions on your behalf. These delegates are incentivized to act honestly because they can be voted out if they misbehave.

Benefits of DPoS:

- Higher efficiency: With a limited number of delegates responsible for block production, DPoS can achieve faster transaction speeds and higher throughput compared to traditional PoS.
- Reduced energy consumption: DPoS generally consumes less energy than PoW because it doesn't require computationally intensive mining.
- Increased flexibility: DPoS allows for more flexibility in governance and decision-making, as delegates can be easily voted in or out.

Examples of DPoS blockchains:

- EOS
- Steem
- Bitshares

2. Practical Byzantine Fault Tolerance (PBFT)

PBFT is a consensus mechanism designed to be highly fault-tolerant. This means it can continue to operate correctly even if some nodes in the network are malicious or faulty.

It works by having nodes exchange messages and vote on the validity of transactions and blocks. As long as a certain threshold of honest nodes agree, the system can continue to function securely.

Benefits of PBFT:

- High fault tolerance: Can handle a significant number of faulty or malicious nodes without compromising the network's integrity.
- Finality: Transactions are considered final once they are included in a block, eliminating the need for confirmations.

Examples of PBFT blockchains:

- Hyperledger Fabric
- Quorum

3. Proof-of-Authority (PoA)

PoA relies on a set of authorized validators who are responsible for adding blocks to the chain. These validators are typically pre-selected and trusted entities.

This mechanism is often used in private or consortium blockchains where a limited number of known participants need to maintain a high degree of control and efficiency.

Benefits of PoA:

- High efficiency: With a limited number of trusted validators, PoA can achieve high transaction throughput and low latency.
- Simplified governance: The pre-selected validators simplify the governance process.

Examples of PoA blockchains:

- VeChain
- POA Network

4. Directed Acyclic Graph (DAG)

DAG is a different approach to blockchain architecture that uses a directed acyclic graph instead of a linear chain of blocks. In a DAG, transactions are linked to each other directly, forming a web-like structure.

This can lead to higher scalability and faster transaction speeds because transactions don't need to wait for block confirmations. However, DAG-based systems can be more complex to implement and secure.

Examples of DAG-based blockchains:

- IOTA
- Nano

Choosing the Right Consensus Mechanism

Selecting the appropriate consensus mechanism for your blockchain project depends on various factors:

- Security requirements: How crucial is it to prevent malicious attacks and ensure data integrity?
- Scalability needs: How many transactions per second does the blockchain need to handle?
- Energy efficiency: How much energy consumption is acceptable?
- Network type: Is it a public, private, or permissioned blockchain?
- Governance model: How will decisions be made on the network?

Go and Consensus Mechanisms

While Go might not be the language used to implement the core consensus algorithms of these blockchains, it can be used to build tools and applications that interact with them. For example, you could use Go to:

- Build block explorers: Applications that allow users to browse and search the blockchain data.
- Create monitoring tools: Monitor the health and performance of the blockchain network.
- Develop wallets: Allow users to store and manage their digital assets.
- Build decentralized applications (DApps): Interact with smart contracts and the blockchain to provide decentralized services.

By understanding the different consensus mechanisms and their trade-offs, you gain a deeper understanding of how blockchains work and can make informed decisions when designing and building your own blockchain applications.

7.2 Understanding State Channels and Off-Chain Solutions

As blockchain technology gains traction, one of the biggest challenges it faces is scalability.[1] Simply put, how can we make blockchains faster and more efficient to handle a growing number of transactions?

That's where state channels and off-chain solutions come into play. They offer innovative ways to improve blockchain scalability without compromising security or decentralization.[2]

Think of a state channel as a private "room" off the main blockchain where two or more parties can transact directly with each other. It's like having a separate conversation away from the main crowd.

Here's how it works:

1. Opening the Channel: Participants create a multi-signature wallet (a wallet that requires multiple signatures to

authorize transactions) and deposit some funds into it.[3] This transaction is recorded on the blockchain.

2. Transacting Off-Chain: Participants can now transact freely with each other within the channel. These transactions are not broadcast to the main blockchain, but they are signed by all participants to ensure validity.[4]

3. Closing the Channel: When the participants are finished transacting, they close the channel.[5] The final state of the channel (e.g., the final balances of each participant) is then recorded on the main blockchain.[6]

Benefits of State Channels:

- Increased Speed: Transactions within a state channel are incredibly fast because they don't need to be confirmed by the entire blockchain network.[7]
- Reduced Costs: You only pay transaction fees when opening and closing the channel, not for each individual transaction within the channel.[8] This can significantly reduce costs, especially for applications with frequent interactions.[9]
- Improved Privacy: Transactions within a state channel are not publicly visible on the blockchain, providing increased privacy for participants.[10]
- Scalability: State channels allow for a large number of transactions to occur off-chain, reducing the burden on the main blockchain and improving overall scalability.[11]

Real-World Examples of State Channels:

- Payment channels: Used for micropayments and frequent transactions, such as paying for in-game items or streaming services.
- Gaming: Enabling fast and low-cost interactions within games, such as trading in-game assets or making bets.[12]
- Decentralized exchanges: Facilitating faster and cheaper trades between users.[13]

Off-Chain Solutions

State channels are just one type of off-chain solution. Other approaches include:

- Sidechains: Separate blockchains that are interoperable with the main blockchain.[14] They allow for experimentation with new features and scalability solutions without affecting the main chain.
- Plasma: A framework for creating child blockchains that periodically submit their state to the main chain.[15] This allows for increased scalability and complex computations off-chain.
- Rollups: Techniques for bundling multiple transactions off-chain and submitting a single proof to the main chain.[16] This reduces the amount of data that needs to be stored on the main chain, improving efficiency.

Go and Off-Chain Solutions

Go can be used to build applications that interact with and manage state channels and other off-chain solutions.[17] For example, you could use Go to:

- Create wallets: Develop wallets that support state channel transactions, allowing users to open, manage, and close channels.
- Build state channel hubs: Create services that facilitate the creation and management of state channels between users.
- Develop applications that utilize off-chain solutions: Build DApps that leverage sidechains, Plasma, or rollups to improve scalability and efficiency.

Example: A Simple Payment Channel (Conceptual)

While a full implementation of a state channel is complex, here's a conceptual example of how you might represent a simple payment channel in Go:

```Go
type PaymentChannel struct {

    ChannelID        string

    Participants     []string

    Balances         map[string]int

    Nonce            int

    ClosingTxHash string

}
```

This PaymentChannel struct holds information about the channel, including the participants, their balances, a nonce (to prevent replay attacks), and the hash of the closing transaction.

State channels and off-chain solutions are essential tools for addressing scalability challenges in blockchain technology.[18] They offer innovative ways to increase transaction speed, reduce costs, and improve privacy without compromising the core benefits of decentralization and security.[19]

7.3 Implementing Advanced Cryptography Techniques

We've already explored some fundamental cryptography concepts like hash functions and digital signatures, which are essential building blocks for blockchain technology. Now, let's push the boundaries further and explore some advanced cryptographic techniques that can enhance the security, privacy, and functionality of your blockchain applications.

1. Zero-Knowledge Proofs (ZKPs)

Zero-knowledge proofs (ZKPs) are a fascinating cryptographic technique that allows you to prove that you know something without revealing the information itself. It's like proving you have a key to a locked box without actually showing the key or opening the box.

Here's a simplified example:

Let's say you want to prove to someone that you know the solution to a Sudoku puzzle without revealing the actual solution. You could use a ZKP to do this. The ZKP would convince the other person that you know the solution without them seeing the solved puzzle.

How ZKPs work:

ZKPs involve two parties: a prover and a verifier. The prover wants to prove to the verifier that they possess certain knowledge or have performed a specific computation without revealing the details.

The process typically involves a series of interactions between the prover and the verifier, where the prover provides evidence that convinces the verifier of the claim without disclosing the underlying information.

Benefits of ZKPs:

- Enhanced privacy: You can prove things without revealing sensitive information.
- Improved security: ZKPs can be used to authenticate users and verify transactions without exposing private keys or other sensitive data.
- Increased efficiency: ZKPs can reduce the amount of data that needs to be transmitted and processed, improving efficiency.

Real-world examples of ZKPs:

- Zcash: A privacy-focused cryptocurrency that uses ZKPs to shield transaction details.
- Filecoin: A decentralized storage network that uses ZKPs to prove that storage providers are storing data correctly.
- Identity verification: ZKPs can be used to verify your identity without revealing your personal information.

Go and ZKPs:

Go provides libraries that support the implementation of ZKPs. Some popular options include:

- gnark: A Go library for building and using zero-knowledge proof systems.
- zokrates: A toolbox for zkSNARKs (a type of ZKP) that can be integrated with Go applications.

2. Homomorphic Encryption

Homomorphic encryption is another powerful cryptographic technique that allows you to perform computations on encrypted data without decrypting it. It's like performing surgery on a patient without ever opening them up.

How homomorphic encryption works:

You can encrypt data using a homomorphic encryption scheme and then perform computations on the encrypted data. The result of the computation, when decrypted, will be the same as if you had performed the computation on the original unencrypted data.

Benefits of homomorphic encryption:

- Secure data processing: You can process sensitive data without exposing it in its unencrypted form.
- Privacy-preserving computations: Perform computations on data without revealing the data itself.

- Secure data sharing: Share encrypted data with others, allowing them to perform computations on it without compromising confidentiality.

Real-world examples of homomorphic encryption:

- Secure cloud computing: Process sensitive data in the cloud without decrypting it.
- Private machine learning: Train machine learning models on encrypted data without accessing the raw data.
- Secure voting systems: Tally votes without revealing individual votes.

Go and homomorphic encryption:

While Go doesn't have extensive built-in support for homomorphic encryption, there are third-party libraries and tools that you can integrate with your Go applications.

3. Other Advanced Cryptography Techniques

Other advanced cryptography techniques relevant to blockchain include:

- Threshold cryptography: Distributes cryptographic keys among multiple parties to prevent single points of failure and enhance security.
- Multi-party computation (MPC): Allows multiple parties to jointly compute a function on their private inputs without revealing their inputs to each other.
- Ring signatures: Allow a member of a group to sign a message on behalf of the group without revealing their individual identity.

Go and Advanced Cryptography

As you continue exploring blockchain development with Go, you can research and experiment with these advanced cryptography techniques. Go provides a flexible and powerful platform for implementing and integrating these technologies into your blockchain applications.

Chapter 8: Deploying Your Blockchain Application

This chapter will guide you through the process of deploying your blockchain application, from choosing the right platform to setting up a network.

8.1 Choosing a Deployment Platform

Congratulations on reaching this stage! You've built your blockchain application, and now it's time to make it accessible to the world. This crucial step involves choosing the right deployment platform – the environment where your application will live and operate.

Think of it like choosing the right foundation for a house. You wouldn't build a skyscraper on a weak foundation, right? Similarly, choosing the right deployment platform is essential for the stability, security, and scalability of your blockchain application.

Factors to Consider

Selecting the optimal deployment platform requires careful consideration of several factors:

Type of Blockchain

- Public: If you're building a public blockchain application, like a decentralized exchange or a cryptocurrency wallet, you'll need a platform that can handle a large number of users and transactions. Public cloud platforms or specialized blockchain platforms might be suitable options.
- Private: For private blockchains, often used within organizations for internal processes, you might choose to deploy on-premises or use a permissioned blockchain platform with access control features.

- Permissioned: Consortium blockchains, where a group of organizations collaborate, often require platforms that provide a balance of privacy and accessibility. Cloud platforms with permissioned blockchain services or specialized consortium blockchain platforms can be good choices.

Scalability Needs

- Transaction Volume: How many transactions per second does your application need to handle? If you anticipate a high volume, you'll need a platform that can scale accordingly. Cloud platforms or high-performance blockchain platforms are often suitable for this.
- Data Storage: How much data will your application generate and store? Consider platforms with efficient and scalable storage solutions, especially if you're dealing with large datasets.

Security Requirements

- Data Privacy: How sensitive is the data handled by your application? If you're dealing with confidential information, prioritize platforms with strong security measures, such as encryption and access control.
- Attack Resistance: Blockchain applications can be vulnerable to various attacks. Choose a platform that provides security features like network monitoring, intrusion detection, and secure key management.

Cost

- Infrastructure Costs: Evaluate the cost of servers, storage, and bandwidth for different platforms. Cloud platforms often offer pay-as-you-go models, which can be more cost-effective than on-premises deployments.

- Transaction Fees: Some blockchain platforms have transaction fees. Factor these fees into your cost analysis, especially if your application involves frequent transactions.

Control and Management

- Infrastructure Control: Do you need full control over the underlying infrastructure, or are you comfortable with a managed solution? On-premises deployments offer more control, while cloud platforms and BaaS solutions provide managed services.
- Maintenance: Consider the level of maintenance required for different platforms. Cloud platforms often handle infrastructure maintenance, while on-premises deployments require you to manage it yourself.

Deployment Options

Let's explore some common deployment options in more detail:

Cloud Platforms:

- AWS, Azure, Google Cloud: These major cloud providers offer a range of blockchain-specific services, including managed blockchain platforms, ledger databases, and developer tools. They provide scalability, reliability, and pay-as-you-go pricing models.
- Examples: Deploying a Hyperledger Fabric network on AWS using Amazon Managed Blockchain, running an Ethereum node on Azure using Azure Blockchain Service.

On-Premises:

- Your Own Servers: You can deploy your blockchain application on servers that you own and manage. This gives you maximum control over the infrastructure but requires technical expertise and resources for setup, maintenance, and security.

- Examples: Setting up a private Ethereum network within a company's data center, deploying a Hyperledger Fabric network on dedicated servers.

Hybrid:

- Combination of Cloud and On-Premises: You can combine cloud and on-premises deployments to leverage the benefits of both. For example, you might use a cloud platform for scalability and on-premises servers for sensitive data or critical components.
- Examples: Running some nodes of a blockchain network on a cloud platform and others on-premises, using a cloud platform for development and testing and on-premises for production.

Blockchain-as-a-Service (BaaS):

- Managed Blockchain Platforms: BaaS providers offer managed blockchain platforms that simplify deployment and management. They handle infrastructure setup, maintenance, and security, allowing you to focus on your application development.
- Examples: Using Kaleido to deploy and manage a consortium blockchain, using Block Daemon to run an Ethereum node.

Choosing the right deployment platform is a crucial decision that can significantly impact the success of your blockchain application. Carefully consider your needs and priorities, evaluate the different options, and choose the platform that provides the best balance of scalability, security, cost, and control for your specific use case.

8.2 Deploying to Cloud Platforms

Cloud platforms have become a popular choice for deploying blockchain applications. They offer numerous advantages, including scalability, reliability, and a wide range of services tailored for blockchain development. Let's explore how you can deploy your blockchain application to some of the leading cloud platforms: AWS, Azure, and Google Cloud.

Why Choose Cloud Platforms for Blockchain Deployment?

Here are some compelling reasons to consider cloud platforms for your blockchain application:

- Scalability: Cloud platforms allow you to easily scale your resources up or down based on your needs. This is crucial for blockchain applications that may experience fluctuating demand.
- Reliability: Cloud providers offer high availability and fault tolerance, ensuring your application remains accessible even in the face of hardware failures or network issues.
- Security: Cloud platforms provide robust security measures, including encryption, access control, and network security, to protect your application and data.
- Cost-effectiveness: You typically pay only for the resources you use, making cloud platforms a cost-effective option, especially for smaller projects or applications with variable workloads.
- Ease of use: Cloud providers offer user-friendly interfaces and tools that simplify the deployment and management of your blockchain application.
- Managed Services: Many cloud providers offer managed blockchain services that take care of the underlying infrastructure, allowing you to focus on your application logic.

AWS (Amazon Web Services)

AWS provides a comprehensive suite of services for blockchain development and deployment:

- Amazon Managed Blockchain: This fully managed service allows you to create and manage blockchain networks using popular frameworks like Hyperledger Fabric and Ethereum. It handles tasks like node provisioning, software updates, and security, simplifying network management.
- Amazon Quantum Ledger Database (QLDB): This is a ledger database that provides a transparent, immutable, and cryptographically verifiable transaction log. It's suitable for applications that require an auditable history of transactions, such as supply chain management or financial record-keeping.
- AWS Blockchain Templates: AWS offers pre-built templates that simplify the deployment of popular blockchain frameworks. These templates provide a starting point for your deployment, allowing you to quickly set up a blockchain network without having to configure everything from scratch.

Azure (Microsoft Azure)

Azure also offers a variety of services for blockchain deployment:

- Azure Blockchain Service: This fully managed service allows you to create and manage consortium blockchain networks. It supports popular frameworks like Quorum, Corda, and Hyperledger Fabric, and provides features like built-in governance and access control.
- Azure Confidential Ledger: This is a highly secure, tamper-proof ledger for storing sensitive data. It uses specialized hardware and cryptographic techniques to protect data confidentiality and integrity.

- Azure Blockchain Workbench: This is a collection of tools and services that simplify the development and deployment of blockchain applications. It provides pre-built templates, sample code, and development environments to accelerate your blockchain projects.

Google Cloud (Google Cloud Platform)

Google Cloud offers its own set of blockchain services:

- Google Cloud Blockchain Platform: This fully managed service allows you to build and deploy blockchain applications using various frameworks. It provides features like node management, smart contract deployment, and network monitoring.
- BigQuery: This is a fully managed, serverless data warehouse that can be used to analyze blockchain data. You can use BigQuery to query and analyze large datasets of blockchain transactions and extract valuable insights.
- Cloud Spanner: This is a globally distributed, scalable database that can be used for blockchain data storage. It offers high availability, consistency, and security for your blockchain data.

General Steps for Cloud Deployment

While the specific steps may vary depending on the chosen cloud provider and blockchain service, here's a general outline of the deployment process:

1. Select a Service: Choose the appropriate blockchain service from your chosen cloud provider based on your needs and the type of blockchain you're using.
2. Create a Blockchain Network: Configure the network settings, such as the number of nodes, consensus mechanism, and access control rules.

3. Provision Infrastructure: The cloud provider will typically handle the provisioning of the necessary infrastructure, such as virtual machines, storage, and networking.
4. Deploy Smart Contracts: Deploy your smart contracts to the blockchain network using the provided tools or APIs.
5. Connect Your Application: Connect your frontend application to the blockchain network using the appropriate libraries and APIs.
6. Configure Security: Set up access control, encryption, and other security measures to protect your application and data.
7. Monitor and Maintain: Monitor the health and performance of your blockchain network and perform regular maintenance tasks as needed.

Real-World Examples

- Supply Chain Management: A company uses AWS Managed Blockchain to deploy a Hyperledger Fabric network for tracking goods across its supply chain, improving transparency and efficiency.
- Financial Services: A bank uses Azure Blockchain Service to create a consortium network for secure and efficient interbank transactions, reducing costs and settlement times.
- Healthcare: A healthcare provider uses Google Cloud Blockchain Platform to store and share patient data securely on a blockchain, ensuring data privacy and interoperability.

By understanding the various cloud platforms and their blockchain services, you can make informed decisions about where to deploy your application. Remember to consider factors like scalability, security, cost, and ease of use when choosing a platform.

8.3 Setting Up a Blockchain Network

While cloud platforms and BaaS solutions offer convenient ways to deploy blockchain applications, setting up your own network gives you greater control over the infrastructure and configuration. This can be particularly beneficial if you have specific security or performance requirements or if you need to maintain complete control over your data.

Steps to Set Up a Blockchain Network

Choose a Consensus Mechanism

The consensus mechanism is the heart of your blockchain network. It determines how nodes agree on the validity of transactions and the order of blocks. Consider factors like security, scalability, and energy efficiency when making your choice.

Some popular consensus mechanisms include:

- Proof-of-Work (PoW): Used in Bitcoin, PoW requires miners to solve complex mathematical problems to add blocks to the chain. It's highly secure but energy-intensive.
- Proof-of-Stake (PoS): Used in Ethereum (after the Merge), PoS allows validators to stake their cryptocurrency to participate in block production. It's more energy-efficient than PoW.
- Delegated Proof-of-Stake (DPoS): Token holders vote for delegates who validate transactions and produce blocks. This can lead to faster transaction speeds.
- Practical Byzantine Fault Tolerance (PBFT): Highly fault-tolerant, suitable for permissioned blockchains.

Set Up Nodes

A blockchain network consists of multiple nodes, each running the blockchain software and maintaining a copy of the blockchain data. You'll need to set up at least one node, but multiple nodes are recommended for redundancy and fault tolerance.

Here's a general outline of the node setup process:

- Choose your hardware: Select servers or virtual machines with sufficient processing power, memory, and storage to handle the blockchain workload.
- Install the blockchain software: Download and install the software for your chosen blockchain platform (e.g., geth for Ethereum, go-ethereum for Go).
- Configure the node: Configure network settings, such as IP addresses, ports, and firewall rules.
- Start the node: Run the blockchain software to start the node.

Configure the Network

Once you have your nodes set up, you need to configure the network to enable communication and data synchronization between them.

- Network topology: Decide on the network topology (e.g., peer-to-peer, hub-and-spoke).
- Network discovery: Configure how nodes discover each other on the network.
- Data synchronization: Ensure that nodes can synchronize their blockchain data efficiently.

Join Nodes to the Network

Connect the nodes to form a network. This typically involves configuring each node to connect to other nodes in the network.

For example, in Ethereum, you would use the admin.addPeer() function in geth to connect to other nodes.

Initialize the Blockchain

Once the network is established, you need to initialize the blockchain. This involves creating the genesis block, the first block in the chain. The process for initializing the blockchain varies depending on the blockchain platform. For example, in Ethereum, you would use the `geth init` command to initialize a new blockchain with a genesis file.

Key Considerations for Network Setup

- Security: Implement robust security measures to protect your network from attacks. This includes securing your nodes, using strong passwords, and keeping your software up to date.
- Scalability: Design your network to handle the expected transaction volume and data growth. This might involve using techniques like sharding or off-chain solutions.
- Performance: Optimize network settings for optimal performance. This includes configuring network bandwidth, block size, and consensus parameters.
- Monitoring: Set up monitoring tools to track the health and performance of your network. This allows you to identify and address any issues proactively.

Go and Network Setup

Go can be a valuable tool for automating the process of setting up and managing your blockchain network. You can use Go to:

- Create scripts: Automate the installation and configuration of blockchain software on nodes.
- Develop monitoring tools: Monitor the health and performance of the network, track key metrics, and alert you to potential problems.
- Build management dashboards: Provide a user interface for managing your network, including adding and removing nodes, configuring settings, and monitoring activity.

Real-World Example

A group of financial institutions collaborates to create a permissioned blockchain network for secure data sharing. They set up their own network using Hyperledger Fabric, deploy nodes on their respective servers, and configure the network with appropriate access control rules. They use Go to develop tools for monitoring the network and managing user permissions.

By understanding the steps involved in setting up a blockchain network and leveraging the power of Go for automation and management, you can create a robust and efficient blockchain infrastructure tailored to your specific needs.

Chapter 9: Security and Best Practices

You've built your blockchain application, chosen a deployment platform, and are ready to share it with the world. But before you do, let's take a crucial step back and focus on security and best practices. Think of security as the immune system of your blockchain application. Just like our bodies need defenses against viruses and bacteria, your application needs protection against malicious attacks and vulnerabilities.

9.1 Common Security Vulnerabilities

While blockchain technology itself offers inherent security features like immutability and decentralization, it's important to remember that blockchain *applications* can still be vulnerable to various security risks.[1] Think of it like a fortress with strong walls – the fortress itself might be sturdy, but if the gates are left open or there are weaknesses in the design, attackers can still find ways to breach it.

Let's explore some common security vulnerabilities that can affect blockchain applications:

1. Smart Contract Vulnerabilities

Smart contracts are the heart of many blockchain applications, but they can be susceptible to various vulnerabilities if not carefully designed and implemented.[2]

- Reentrancy Attacks: This type of attack exploits a vulnerability in a smart contract that allows an attacker to repeatedly call a function before the first call is completed.[3] This can be used to drain funds from a contract or manipulate its state.[4]

Example: A vulnerable contract might have a function to withdraw funds. An attacker could create a malicious contract that calls this withdraw function, and within that function, call the withdraw function again before the first call completes.[5] This can be repeated multiple times, draining the vulnerable contract's funds.[6]

- Logic Errors: Bugs or flaws in the logic of a smart contract can lead to unexpected behavior and vulnerabilities.[7] These errors can be as simple as incorrect calculations or more complex logic flaws that allow attackers to exploit the contract.

Example: A contract might have a logic error that allows an attacker to bypass access control checks or withdraw more funds than they are entitled to.[8]

- Integer Overflow/Underflow: Integers in computer programs have a maximum and minimum value.[9] If an arithmetic operation results in a value that exceeds these limits, it can "wrap around," leading to an integer overflow or underflow. This can cause unexpected behavior and vulnerabilities in smart contracts.

Example: A contract might use an unsigned integer to store a balance. If an attacker can cause an underflow by subtracting a large amount from the balance, the balance could wrap around to a very large number, allowing the attacker to withdraw more funds than they should have.[10]

2. Key Management Issues

The security of blockchain applications heavily relies on the proper management of cryptographic keys.[11]

- Private Key Compromise: A user's private key is like their digital identity and controls access to their funds and assets on the blockchain.[12] If an attacker gains access to a user's private key, they can impersonate the user and steal their assets.[13]

Example: An attacker might use phishing techniques to trick a user into revealing their private key or exploit a vulnerability in a wallet software to steal the key.[14]

- Weak Key Generation: If private keys are generated using weak random number generators, they might be predictable and vulnerable to brute-force attacks, where an attacker tries to guess the key by trying many different possibilities.

Example: Using a poorly designed random number generator could result in private keys that are clustered within a certain range, making it easier for an attacker to guess them.

3. Network Attacks

Blockchain networks themselves can be vulnerable to certain types of attacks.

- 51% Attacks: In blockchains that use Proof-of-Work (PoW), if a single entity gains control of more than 50% of the network's hashing power, they can potentially double-spend coins, reverse transactions, or even alter the blockchain's history.[15]

Example: A group of miners could collude to control a majority of the network's hash rate and then use this power to double-spend their coins or prevent other users' transactions from being confirmed.[16]

- Denial-of-Service (DoS) Attacks: Attackers can flood a blockchain network with traffic, overwhelming its resources and preventing legitimate users from accessing the network or processing transactions.[17]

Example: An attacker could send a large number of invalid transactions or requests to the network, causing congestion and preventing legitimate transactions from being processed.

4. Phishing and Social Engineering

Attackers often target users directly through social engineering and phishing attacks.

- Phishing Attacks: These attacks involve tricking users into revealing their private keys or other sensitive information through fake websites, emails, or messages that appear to be from legitimate sources.[18]

Example: An attacker might create a fake website that looks like a popular cryptocurrency exchange and trick users into entering their login credentials, which the attacker can then use to steal their funds.[19]

- Social Engineering: Attackers use psychological manipulation to trick users into performing actions that compromise their security, such as downloading malware, revealing passwords, or sending funds to fraudulent addresses.[20]

Example: An attacker might impersonate a customer support representative and convince a user to provide their private key or seed phrase to "recover their account."

Understanding these vulnerabilities is the first step towards mitigating them. In the next section, we'll explore best practices for secure development and how to protect your blockchain applications from these threats.

9.2 Best Practices for Secure Development

Now that you're aware of the common security vulnerabilities that can plague blockchain applications, let's shift our focus to best practices for secure development. Think of these as the proactive measures you can take to build a robust and resilient application, minimizing the risk of attacks and vulnerabilities.

1. Secure Smart Contract Development

Smart contracts are often the most critical component of a blockchain application, so securing them is paramount. Here are some key practices to follow:

- Formal Verification: This involves using mathematical techniques to rigorously prove the correctness of your smart contract code. Formal verification tools can help identify potential vulnerabilities and ensure that your contract behaves as intended under all conditions.
- Code Audits: Having experienced security auditors review your code is crucial for identifying vulnerabilities that you might have missed. Auditors can provide valuable insights and recommendations for improving the security of your contracts.
- Secure Coding Practices: Adhere to secure coding guidelines specific to the smart contract language you're using (e.g., Solidity, Vyper). These guidelines often include recommendations for preventing common vulnerabilities like reentrancy attacks, integer overflows, and access control issues.

Example (Solidity):

```
Solidity

pragma solidity ^0.8.0;

contract SecureTransfer {

    mapping(address => uint256) public balances;
```

```solidity
    // Use a modifier to prevent reentrancy
attacks

    modifier nonReentrant() {

        require(!_isReentrant, "Reentrancy attack
detected");

        _isReentrant = true;

        _;

        _isReentrant = false;

    }

    bool private _isReentrant = false;

    function transfer(address _to, uint256
_amount) public nonReentrant {

        require(balances[msg.sender] >= _amount,
"Insufficient balance");

        balances[msg.sender] -= _amount;

        balances[_to] += _amount;

    }

}
```

In this example, the nonReentrant modifier is used to prevent reentrancy attacks by using a boolean flag (_isReentrant) to track whether the function is currently being executed.

- Use Established Libraries: When possible, leverage well-tested and audited libraries for common functionalities like token implementations, mathematical operations, and access control. This can reduce the risk of introducing vulnerabilities through your own code.

2. Robust Key Management

Protecting private keys is crucial for securing user assets and preventing unauthorized access.

- Secure Key Storage: Use secure methods to store private keys, such as:
    - Hardware Wallets: These are dedicated devices designed for secure key storage and transaction signing.
    - Secure Key Management Systems: These systems provide secure storage, access control, and management of cryptographic keys.
- Multi-Signature Wallets: For applications that require high security, consider using multi-signature wallets, which require multiple parties to approve a transaction before it can be executed. This reduces the risk of a single compromised key leading to the loss of funds.

3. Network Security

Securing the network infrastructure is essential for preventing attacks and ensuring the availability of your blockchain application.

- Node Security: Harden your blockchain nodes by:
    - Keeping the node software up to date with the latest security patches.
    - Using firewalls to restrict incoming and outgoing network traffic.
    - Implementing intrusion detection systems to monitor for suspicious activity.
    - Regularly backing up your node data.
- Network Monitoring: Continuously monitor your network for suspicious activity, such as unusual transaction patterns or attempts to compromise nodes. Use monitoring tools to

track key metrics and receive alerts for potential security breaches.

4. User Education

User education plays a vital role in security. Empower your users to protect themselves by:

- Security Awareness: Educate users about common security threats, such as phishing attacks, social engineering, and malware. Provide clear and concise information about how to protect their accounts and assets.
- Phishing Prevention: Train users to recognize and avoid phishing attempts. Encourage them to be cautious of suspicious emails, messages, and websites that ask for their private keys or other sensitive information.
- Best Practices: Promote best practices for password management, software updates, and secure device usage.

Real-World Examples

- The QuadrigaCX Case: A Canadian cryptocurrency exchange collapsed in 2019 after its CEO, who was the sole custodian of the private keys, died unexpectedly. This highlighted the risks of centralized key management and the importance of multi-signature wallets or secure key management systems.
- The Mt. Gox Hack: One of the largest Bitcoin exchanges was hacked in 2014, resulting in the loss of hundreds of thousands of Bitcoins. This incident emphasized the importance of robust network security and the need for continuous monitoring and security audits.

By implementing these best practices and prioritizing security throughout the development lifecycle, you can significantly reduce the risk of vulnerabilities and build secure and trustworthy blockchain applications. Remember that security is an ongoing effort, and it's essential to stay vigilant, adapt to evolving threats, and continuously improve your security posture.

9.3 Testing and Auditing

In the world of blockchain, where transactions are irreversible and smart contracts are immutable, even small errors can have significant consequences. Thorough testing and auditing help you:

- Identify and fix bugs: Uncover errors and unexpected behavior in your code before they cause problems in production.
- Improve code quality: Ensure your code is well-structured, maintainable, and efficient.
- Enhance security: Identify and mitigate vulnerabilities that could be exploited by attackers.
- Build trust and confidence: Demonstrate to users and stakeholders that your application is reliable and secure.

Testing Your Blockchain Code

Testing involves systematically executing your code to identify any discrepancies between expected and actual behavior. Here are some common types of testing for blockchain applications:

- **Unit Testing:** This focuses on testing individual units or components of your code in isolation. For example, you might write unit tests for specific functions in your smart contracts or for individual modules in your Go backend code.

Example (Go):

```Go

package main
```

```go
import "testing"

func add(x int, y int) int {

    return x + y

}

func TestAdd(t *testing.T) {

    result := add(2, 3)

    if result != 5 {

        t.Errorf("add(2, 3) = %d; want 5",
result)

    }

}
```

This Go code defines a simple add function and a TestAdd function that tests the add function with specific inputs and checks if the output matches the expected result.

- Integration Testing: This involves testing the interaction between different components of your application. For example, you might test how your Go backend interacts with your smart contracts or how different smart contracts interact with each other.
- End-to-End Testing: This tests the entire application flow from the user interface to the blockchain. It simulates real-world user interactions and verifies that the application behaves as expected.

Auditing Your Blockchain Code

While testing focuses on identifying functional errors and unexpected behavior, auditing goes deeper into the code to assess its security and identify potential vulnerabilities.

- Smart Contract Audits: Engage experienced security auditors to thoroughly review your smart contract code. They will analyze the code for vulnerabilities like reentrancy attacks, logic errors, and integer overflows. Auditors will provide a detailed report with their findings and recommendations for remediation.
- Security Audits: Conduct comprehensive security audits of your entire application, including the infrastructure, network, and application code. This helps identify vulnerabilities in all aspects of your system and provides a holistic view of your security posture.

Tools and Techniques for Testing and Auditing

- Testing Frameworks: Go provides built-in testing frameworks and third-party libraries like testify that can help you write comprehensive tests.
- Static Analysis Tools: These tools analyze your code without executing it, helping identify potential vulnerabilities and code smells. Examples include go vet and golint.
- Dynamic Analysis Tools: These tools analyze your code during execution, helping identify runtime vulnerabilities and performance issues.
- Fuzzing: This technique involves providing random or unexpected inputs to your code to uncover vulnerabilities that might not be found through traditional testing methods.

Real-World Examples

- The Parity Multi-Sig Wallet Vulnerability: A vulnerability in the Parity multi-signature wallet, discovered through an audit, allowed an attacker to drain millions of dollars worth of Ether in 2017. This incident highlighted the importance of thorough code audits and the need to address vulnerabilities promptly.

- The DAO Hack: A vulnerability in the DAO's smart contract code, which was not identified through adequate testing and auditing, led to a massive exploit in 2016, resulting in the loss of millions of dollars. This event emphasized the critical role of testing and auditing in preventing costly security breaches.

By incorporating rigorous testing and auditing practices into your development process, you can significantly improve the quality, security, and reliability of your blockchain applications.

Chapter 10: The Future of Blockchain with Go

We've covered a lot of ground in this book, from the fundamentals of blockchain to building DApps and exploring advanced concepts. Now, let's look ahead and explore the exciting future of blockchain with Go

10.1 Emerging Trends in Blockchain Technology

The blockchain space is a dynamic and rapidly evolving field. New ideas, innovations, and trends are constantly emerging, pushing the boundaries of what's possible with this technology. As a developer, it's essential to stay informed about these trends to build cutting-edge applications and contribute to the future of blockchain.

1. Layer-2 Scaling Solutions

One of the biggest challenges facing blockchain technology is scalability – the ability to handle a large number of transactions efficiently.[1] As blockchain adoption grows, networks can become congested, leading to slower transaction speeds and higher fees.[2]

Layer-2 scaling solutions aim to address this challenge by moving transactions off the main blockchain (Layer-1) to a secondary layer (Layer-2).[3] This allows for faster and cheaper transactions while still leveraging the security and decentralization of the main blockchain.[4]

Some popular Layer-2 solutions include:

- State Channels: We discussed state channels in Chapter 7. They allow participants to transact directly with each other off-chain, only settling the final result on the main blockchain.[5]

- Sidechains: Separate blockchains that are interoperable with the main blockchain.[6] They can handle a higher volume of transactions and experiment with new features without affecting the main chain.
- Rollups: Techniques for bundling multiple transactions off-chain and submitting a single proof to the main chain.[7] This reduces the amount of data that needs to be processed on the main chain, improving efficiency.

Examples:

- Lightning Network: A Layer-2 solution for Bitcoin that uses payment channels to enable fast and cheap transactions.[8]
- Polygon: A Layer-2 solution for Ethereum that uses a combination of technologies, including Plasma and rollups, to improve scalability.[9]

2. Interoperability

The blockchain ecosystem is becoming increasingly fragmented, with many different blockchains operating independently. Interoperability aims to bridge these isolated networks, allowing for seamless communication and asset transfer between them.[10]

This is like creating a network of interconnected highways between different cities, enabling smooth traffic flow and trade.

Examples:

- Cosmos: A network of interconnected blockchains that can communicate and share data with each other.[11]
- Polkadot: A multi-chain framework that allows different blockchains to interoperate securely.[12]

3. Decentralized Identity

Blockchain technology is enabling new forms of decentralized identity management, giving users more control over their personal data and online identity.[13] This can revolutionize how we authenticate ourselves and interact with online services.

Instead of relying on centralized identity providers (like Google or Facebook), users can control their own digital identities, granting or revoking access to their data as they see fit.

Examples:

- Decentralized Identifiers (DIDs): A new type of identifier that allows users to control their own digital identity.[14]
- Verifiable Credentials: Digital credentials that can be verified cryptographically, providing a secure and trustworthy way to prove identity or attributes.

4. Tokenization

Tokenization is the process of representing real-world assets (like property, stocks, or art) as digital tokens on a blockchain.[15] This can unlock new possibilities for fractional ownership, liquidity, and efficient asset transfer.

For example, a piece of real estate could be tokenized, allowing multiple investors to own a fraction of the property through digital tokens.[16] These tokens can then be traded on a blockchain-based exchange, providing liquidity and fractional ownership.[17]

Examples:

- Security tokens: Representing ownership in a company or asset.[18]
- NFT (Non-Fungible Token): Representing unique digital or physical assets, like collectibles or artwork.[19]

5. Decentralized Autonomous Organizations (DAOs)

DAOs are organizations governed by rules encoded in smart contracts, allowing for decentralized decision-making and autonomous operation.[20] They have the potential to revolutionize how we organize and manage communities and businesses.

In a DAO, members can vote on proposals and decisions, and the outcome is automatically executed by the smart contracts.[21] This eliminates the need for centralized control and allows for more democratic and transparent governance.

Examples:

- MakerDAO: A decentralized organization that manages the Dai stablecoin.[22]
- Uniswap: A decentralized exchange governed by a DAO.[23]

6. The Metaverse and Web3

The metaverse is a persistent, shared virtual world where users can interact with each other and digital assets. Blockchain technology is playing a key role in the development of the metaverse, enabling:

- Ownership of virtual assets: NFTs can represent ownership of virtual land, buildings, and other assets in the metaverse.[24]
- Secure transactions: Cryptocurrencies and blockchain technology can facilitate secure and transparent transactions within the metaverse.[25]
- Decentralized governance: DAOs can be used to govern virtual communities and economies within the metaverse.[26]

Web3 is a vision for a decentralized internet built on blockchain technology.[27] It aims to give users more control over their data and online experiences, reducing reliance on centralized platforms.

Examples:

- Decentraland: A decentralized virtual world platform.[28]

- The Sandbox: A user-generated content platform where users can create and monetize their own gaming experiences.[29]

The blockchain space is constantly evolving, so it's essential to stay informed about the latest trends and innovations. Follow industry publications, attend conferences, and engage with the blockchain community to keep your knowledge up-to-date.

10.2 New Use Cases for Go in Blockchain

Go, with its efficiency, concurrency support, and growing ecosystem, is becoming an increasingly popular language for blockchain development.[1] It's well-suited for building a wide range of blockchain applications, from core infrastructure to decentralized applications (DApps).[2]

Let's explore some exciting new use cases where Go can shine in the blockchain space:

1. Building Scalable Blockchain Infrastructure

As blockchain adoption grows, scalability becomes a critical challenge. Go's efficiency and concurrency features make it an excellent choice for building high-performance blockchain infrastructure that can handle a large volume of transactions and data.

- High-Performance Nodes: Go can be used to develop efficient and reliable blockchain nodes that can process transactions quickly and maintain the integrity of the blockchain.
- Consensus Algorithms: Go's concurrency support makes it well-suited for implementing complex consensus algorithms, such as Proof-of-Stake (PoS) or Delegated Proof-of-Stake (DPoS), which require coordination between multiple nodes.

- Networking Infrastructure: Go's networking libraries and concurrency features can be used to build robust and scalable networking infrastructure for blockchain networks, ensuring efficient communication and data synchronization between nodes.[3]

Example: A blockchain startup uses Go to build a high-performance node implementation for their new Proof-of-Stake blockchain, enabling them to handle a large number of transactions per second and maintain a responsive network.

2. Developing Cross-Chain Interoperability Solutions

Interoperability between different blockchains is becoming increasingly important. Go can be used to develop bridges and protocols that enable communication and asset transfer between different blockchain networks.

- Cross-Chain Bridges: Go can be used to build bridges that connect different blockchains, allowing users to transfer assets and data between them seamlessly.
- Interoperability Protocols: Go can be used to implement interoperability protocols that define standards for communication and data exchange between different blockchains.[4]

Example: A development team uses Go to create a bridge between Ethereum and Cosmos, allowing users to transfer tokens and data between the two networks.

3. Creating Secure Decentralized Identity Systems

Decentralized identity is gaining traction as a way to give users more control over their personal data and online identity.[5] Go can be used to build secure and privacy-preserving decentralized identity solutions.

- Decentralized Identifiers (DIDs): Go can be used to create and manage DIDs, which are globally unique identifiers that allow users to control their own digital identity.[6]
- Verifiable Credentials: Go can be used to issue and verify verifiable credentials, which are digital credentials that can be cryptographically verified, providing a secure and trustworthy way to prove identity or attributes.[7]

Example: A government agency uses Go to develop a decentralized identity system that allows citizens to control their own digital identities and access government services securely.

4. Developing Tools for the Metaverse

The metaverse is a rapidly growing space with a wide range of opportunities for blockchain technology. Go can be used to develop tools and applications for the metaverse, such as:

- Virtual World Clients: Go can be used to build high-performance clients for accessing and interacting with virtual worlds in the metaverse.
- Asset Management Systems: Go can be used to create secure and efficient systems for managing virtual assets, such as NFTs, in the metaverse.
- Decentralized Marketplaces: Go can be used to build decentralized marketplaces for buying, selling, and trading virtual assets in the metaverse.[8]

Example: A gaming company uses Go to develop a virtual world client for their new blockchain-based metaverse game, providing players with a smooth and immersive experience.

5. Building Decentralized Autonomous Organizations (DAOs)

DAOs are becoming increasingly popular as a way to organize and manage communities and businesses in a decentralized manner.[9]

Go can be used to develop the infrastructure and governance mechanisms for DAOs.

- DAO Frameworks: Go can be used to build frameworks for creating and managing DAOs, including tools for voting, proposal submission, and treasury management.
- DAO Governance Mechanisms: Go can be used to implement various DAO governance mechanisms, such as token-weighted voting, quadratic voting, and holographic consensus.

Example: A community of artists uses Go to build a DAO that governs a decentralized platform for showcasing and selling their artwork.

Go's Strengths for Blockchain Development

Go's strengths make it well-suited for these and other blockchain use cases:

- Efficiency: Go's compiled nature and efficient memory management make it ideal for building high-performance blockchain applications.[10]
- Concurrency: Go's built-in concurrency features simplify the development of applications that require parallel processing, such as blockchain nodes and consensus algorithms.
- Strong Ecosystem: Go has a growing ecosystem of libraries and tools for blockchain development, making it easier to build and deploy applications.[11]
- Readability and Maintainability: Go's clear and concise syntax promotes code readability and maintainability, which is crucial for complex blockchain projects.[12]

By exploring these new use cases and leveraging Go's strengths, you can contribute to the growth and innovation of the blockchain ecosystem.

10.3 Resources and Further Learning

The blockchain space is like a constantly expanding universe. New technologies, platforms, and applications are emerging all the time.[1] To stay ahead of the curve and continue growing as a blockchain developer, it's essential to keep learning and exploring.

Think of this section as your roadmap for continued learning and exploration in the blockchain space. It provides a curated list of resources and pathways to help you deepen your knowledge and expand your skill set.

1. Online Courses and Tutorials

Online platforms offer a wealth of knowledge on blockchain technology, Go programming, and smart contract development. These resources can be a great way to learn at your own pace and convenience.

Platforms:

- Coursera: Offers a variety of blockchain-related courses from top universities and institutions.[2]
- edX: Another platform with a wide range of blockchain courses, including introductory and advanced topics.[3]
- Udemy: Provides a vast library of blockchain courses, often with a more practical and hands-on approach.[4]
- Pluralsight: Focuses on technology skills, with a good selection of blockchain and Go programming courses.[5]

Specific Courses to Consider:

- Blockchain Basics: Look for introductory courses that cover the fundamentals of blockchain technology, cryptography, and smart contracts.[6]

- Go Programming: If you're new to Go or want to deepen your knowledge, consider courses that cover Go syntax, data structures, concurrency, and best practices.
- Smart Contract Development: Explore courses that teach you how to write smart contracts using Solidity or other languages, and how to interact with them using Go.
- DApp Development: Look for courses that guide you through the process of building decentralized applications using Go and blockchain technology.[7]

2. Books and Articles

Books and articles provide in-depth knowledge and insights into various aspects of blockchain technology and Go programming.[8]

Blockchain Books:

- "Mastering Bitcoin" by Andreas M. Antonopoulos: A comprehensive guide to Bitcoin technology.[9]
- "Ethereum: Blockchains, Digital Assets, Smart Contracts, DAOs" by Henning Diedrich: A deep dive into the Ethereum ecosystem.[10]
- "Blockchain Basics" by Daniel Drescher: An introductory book that explains blockchain concepts in a clear and accessible way.[11]

Go Programming Books:

- "The Go Programming Language" by Alan A.[12] A. Donovan and Brian W. Kernighan: A classic and comprehensive guide to Go.
- "Effective Go": A document available online that provides best practices and guidelines for writing effective Go code.[13]
- "Concurrency in Go" by Katherine Cox-Buday: Explores Go's concurrency features and how to use them effectively.[14]

Blockchain Articles and Blogs:

- CoinDesk: A leading news and information platform for blockchain and cryptocurrencies.[15]
- Cointelegraph: Another popular source for blockchain news and analysis.[16]
- Medium: Many blockchain experts and developers share their knowledge and insights on Medium.[17]

3. Blockchain Communities and Forums

Engaging with other blockchain enthusiasts and developers can be a valuable way to learn and stay up-to-date.

- Reddit: Subreddits like r/blockchain, r/ethereum, and r/golang provide forums for discussions and sharing information.[18]
- Stack Overflow: A popular platform for asking and answering technical questions related to blockchain and Go.[19]
- Discord: Many blockchain projects and communities have Discord servers where you can connect with other developers and enthusiasts.[20]

4. Open-Source Projects

Contributing to open-source blockchain projects is a great way to gain practical experience and learn from other developers.

- GitHub: Explore blockchain projects on GitHub and contribute to those that interest you.[21]
- Hyperledger Fabric: An open-source enterprise blockchain framework with a vibrant community.[22]
- Ethereum: The Ethereum platform itself is open-source, and you can contribute to its development or to various projects built on Ethereum.[23]

5. Conferences and Meetups

Attending blockchain conferences and meetups allows you to network with other professionals, learn about the latest trends, and gain new perspectives.[24]

- Major Blockchain Conferences: Consensus, Devcon, Bitcoin Conference
- Local Meetups: Search for blockchain meetups in your area to connect with other developers and enthusiasts.

Go-Specific Resources

- The Go Programming Language Website: https://golang.org/ The official website for Go, with documentation, tutorials, and downloads.
- Go Documentation: https://golang.org/doc/ Comprehensive documentation for the Go language and its standard library.
- Go By Example: https://gobyexample.com/ A collection of annotated Go code examples that illustrate various language features and concepts.
- Go Ethereum Library: https://github.com/ethereum/go-ethereum The official Go implementation of the Ethereum protocol.

The blockchain space is constantly evolving, so continuous learning is essential for staying relevant and contributing to this exciting field. Utilize these resources to deepen your knowledge, expand your skills, and connect with the blockchain community.[25]

Conclusion

We've reached the end of our journey through the world of blockchain development with Go. Starting with the fundamental concepts of blockchain, we explored its core components, delved into the intricacies of Go programming, and built our own blockchain applications. We even ventured into advanced topics like smart contracts, decentralized applications, and cutting-edge cryptographic techniques.

Throughout this book, we've emphasized a hands-on approach, providing practical examples and exercises to solidify your understanding. You've learned how to leverage Go's efficiency, concurrency, and robust standard library to build secure, scalable, and innovative blockchain solutions.

But this is just the beginning. The blockchain space is constantly evolving, with new trends and technologies emerging all the time. As you continue your journey, remember to:

- Stay curious: Explore new ideas, experiment with different platforms, and keep learning about the latest advancements in blockchain technology.
- Embrace the community: Engage with other blockchain developers and enthusiasts, share your knowledge, and contribute to open-source projects.
- Prioritize security: Always keep security top of mind, follow best practices, and stay vigilant against potential vulnerabilities.
- Think creatively: Blockchain technology has the potential to revolutionize many industries. Use your skills to build innovative solutions that can solve real-world problems.

Go, with its versatility and growing ecosystem, is well-equipped to play a significant role in the future of blockchain. As you continue to hone your Go programming skills and explore the vast landscape of blockchain technology, you'll be well-positioned to contribute to this exciting and transformative field.

We hope this book has provided you with a solid foundation for your blockchain development journey. Now, go forth and build the decentralized future!

www.ingramcontent.com/pod-product-compliance
Lightning Source LLC
LaVergne TN
LVHW081529050326
832903LV00025B/1694